TALES
of Old
Tonbridge

by Frank Chapman

Froglets Publications Ltd

Brasted Chart,
Westerham,
Kent TN16 ILY

Tel: 01959 562972
Fax: 01959 565365

© Frank Chapman

ISBN: 1 872337 55 4

Front cover illustration:

Tackling a problem at the forge on the Dry Hill corner of Shipbourne Road in 1889 are Mark Coules the blacksmith (in shirtsleeves) assisted by Alfred Thomas Skinner who had a shop opposite the Red Lion pub near the new Public Hall (the Capitol).

Back cover illustration:

Miss Eileen Mallison, a noted Tonbridge artist, painting a scene of Watergate Buildings, demolished in Kent County Council's passion for road widening in the 1960s.

This book was originated by Froglets Publications Ltd and printed and bound by Staples Printers Rochester Ltd, Neptune Close, Medway City Estate, Rochester, Kent ME2 4LT.

Jacket design and additional artwork by Alison Clarke

Contents

How Tunbridge became Tonbridge 6
Great day for the Great Bridge 8
Adam's Ale might be preferred 10
Gracious buildings thrown away 12
Last days on a busy river 14
The streams that vanished 15
Riddle of the Medway cannon 16
The Hartlake Bridge tragedy 18
Old pharmacist's remedies live on 20
When the clock mender called 21
Mr Nice the paraffin man 22
An old-time ironmonger 24
The haberdasher banker 26
Cobbling among the cobwebs 27
Coming of the railway 28
Old monks rest under the railway 32
Steam enthusiast 34
Cool heads prevented a rail
  tragedy 34
Puritan Prude who didn't
  mind a bit 36
Venetian Fete was Tonbridge's
  pride 38
Going to the pictures 40
Great days at the Old Barn 42
Jack's proud car came a cropper 44
Ball workers liked a "snob day" off 46
Why Jack blew out the lantern 47
History in a cloud of dust 48
Mr Uridge had a windmill 50
Tonbridge gets its own newspaper 54
Sunday blast at powder mills 56
Song along the wire 57
Mary's mission to the poor 58
High tide for a new church 60
Twopenny lesson for a pastor 62
New uses for old chapels 64
Sir Charles would never yield 66
The Poor House 68
Reaching for the stars with
  'Lip' Norton 70

Judd second in the great race 71
Queen mother at school's
  400th anniversary 73
School chapel destroyed by fire 74
Funeral horses in dash to Knole 76
New brigade after tragedy 78
The Whitefriars Press disaster 79
Grim tale of secret tunnel 82
Tonbridge in the groove 83
Triple murder in an orchard 84
Cells replaced the old lock-ups 85
Defying the red flag law 86
'Bus war' races for a penny fare 88
Volunteers off to fight the Boer 90
How Sappers spoofed the Turks 92
Playing on the tank and guns 94
Succour for the men of Dunkirk 96
One man's view of great air battle 98
Squatters raid PoW camp 100
Pioneer pilots planned an airfield 102
Men of Kent or Kentish men? 103
Pilot's skill saved airliner 104
Work for the jobless in the
  Great Depression 106
Russian prince who chose
  Tonbridge 108
Family hopping bought new
  clothes 110
Old Thomas hid from the world 112
Pursuit of a fleeing heiress 114
A great love story of 1914 115
Frank Woolley, the Kentish
  Hop Pole 116
The mystery of Devon Loch 120
The night Tonbridge almost
  went under 122
Double triumph for Spender-Clay 124
Len gave the Tories a scare 126
Last days of the Old Town Hall 126

There must be a book in it

MONDAY mornings for the most junior reporter on the *Tonbridge Free Press* before the last war meant a routine known as "doing the vicars". In about a year this duty would pass to a successor. In the meantime our editor "Pop" Doody required his newest recruit to call on every vicar and rector, all Free Church ministers, and pastors of minor chapels recording their news of the past week and noting events to come.

This circuit had to be done on foot or bicycle, Mr Doody rightly insisting that you did not find news riding in buses or cars. Not that we had any cars. He knew there were good stories in churches and never tired of telling us how as a reporter in his home town in Worcestershire interrupted a service by walking up the aisle to tell the vicar that Mafeking had been relieved

Doing the vicars could be usefully combined with visits to pubs for the cribbage and darts results, and an introduction to such minor social graces as accepting a half of mild on the house. Mild, which no longer seems to be available, offered a moderate initiation to beer drinking and was unlikely to alarm one's mother, to whom journalism suggested a future of reckless dissipation.

On the way back posters and notices had to be studied for details of future events to be entered on the office diary. Minor ones such as whist drives could be picked up from the organiser. All others, embracing annual meetings, missionary rallies, fetes, fairs and speeches by visiting politicians and clergy, had to be attended and a report produced for the following week's paper.

With experience it was possible to arrange a swap with a rival reporter from the *Kent and Sussex Courier* — at the risk, it has to be said, of one's inaccuracies arousing the ire of two editors instead of one.

But on no account must a rival reporter be allowed into one's office during the busy time of the week in case he or she stole a glimpse at the all-important diary listing stories in hand.

Rival reporters might meet at the police station for the ritual of the duty sergeant going through the Occurrence Book, and leaving out anything he didn't think you needed to know. It was also acceptable to call together on regular contacts such as Percy Butler at Rex Bentall's smaller shop for details of the Ancient Order of Druids, and Bob Bourner the barber to hear what the RAOB, the "Buffs", had been doing.

In all these ways one got to know Tonbridge and its people, unconsciously accumulating material that might warrant a successor to Arthur H. Neve's *The Tonbridge of Yesterday*. Dozens of copies of this grey-bound volume of 1933 resided on a dusty top shelf in the *Free Press* reporters' cramped office. We ignored them, or occasionally threw them about.

Now I treasure my own well-used and dog-eared copy, a gift from my brother when we started the Ben Botany feature about old Tonbridge in the *Courier* in 1963.

After the *Free Press*, war service, and 12 years in Fleet Street daily journalism I returned to Kent as editor of the *Kent and Sussex Courier* and in time became editorial director of Courier Newspapers. Having always been a writing editor, I made time to produce *The Book of Tonbridge* (1976) and *Tonbridge, Yesterday's Town* (1982). Both proved popular and are now out of print.

Frank Chapman — his two earlier books about Tonbridge are now out of print

Now comes *Tales of Old Tonbridge* suggested by Froglets Publications, a business founded by an old friend and fellow editor Bob Ogley after his "instant" account of the great 1987 storm *In the Wake of The Hurricane* proved a national best-seller.

Since retiring from full-time work in 1988 I have written the Warwick Notebook for the *Courier*. People seem to like it and often send me ideas and photographs, some of which are the basis of stories in this book.

I am grateful to Martin Oxley, Editor of the *Courier*, for permission to reproduce photographs, and to the family of the late Bert Flemons who so generously many years ago gave me permission to publish his old Tonbridge pictures.

The Ben Botany feature, A Window on Tonbridge, which ran in the *Courier* for nine years until 1972 has been another useful source, and I acknowledge particularly contributions over many years by Margaret Blatcher and Gordon Church.

Frank Chapman 1995

How Tunbridge became Tonbridge

TONBRIDGE was Tunbridge until the older spelling was allocated to Tunbridge Wells to avoid confusion, even though the latter town did not exist until the chalybeate springs were discovered in the seventeenth century.

The wells to which wealthy people flocked in search of relief from intestinal disorders were the (Tunbridge) Wells in a wild and undeveloped distant part of the extensive parish administered from our parish church.

In its long history Tonbridge has had many spellings, among them Tonebridge, Tunbrigge and Tonebrig. The original meaning can be only a guess: some said it was Town of Bridges (there used to be five); others favoured a corruption of Dun, meaning a mound or hill fort upon which the original Saxon keep of Tonbridge Castle was built; or Town with a Bridge, to distinguish it from less fortunate places where they had to wade across the river.

In *The Tonbridge of Yesterday* A. H. Neve favours a Saxon derivative, Tun and Burig, the town with a fort.

As the town became established people did not bother too much how it was spelt, Tunbridge and Tonbridge being used according to fancy for hundreds of years. In the mid nineteenth century Tunbridge was generally favoured over Tonbridge, and so it might have gone on had officialdom's tidy mind not intervened when a Local Board was formed in 1870.

This successor to the Vestry had to have a name and Tonbridge was chosen. The South Eastern Railway and the Post Office ignored this and used Tunbridge for the older town, and Tunbridge Wells for its younger more fashionable neighbour up the hill.

The muddle persisted for some twenty years until Neve asked the Local Board to decide — Tunbridge or Tonbridge?

Voting was almost unanimous for the O spelling. So Tonbridge was adopted and over the years everyone fell into line. Not, however, without some well-founded grumbling — still heard today — that the upstart "daughter town" stole our name.

There is a rhyme which goes:

> *We're the Old and Original township, and so*
> *In writing her name Tonbridge uses an O;*
> *Though funny it seems, it's perfectly true*
> *That the daughter town always spells hers with a U*

The Old Town Hall on the corner of Castle Street was demolished in 1901. Its replacement, the new Public Hall (now the Capitol), never fulfilled the same function after the urban district council began meeting at the Castle.

Great day for the Great Bridge

THE main bridge over the Medway below Tonbridge Castle was known as the Great Bridge when it opened with all available pomp and ceremony in September, 1888. Now it is generally known, more modestly, as the Big Bridge.

Bad gradients and narrowness of the old bridge persuaded the Local Board to go for a total replacement as the first stage in its ambitious 20-year High Street improvement programme.

This was not easily achieved. First Bartram's, whose Bridge Brewery across the road was a major Tonbridge industry, had to be persuaded to part with the weatherboarded Castle Inn. Eventually they accepted compensation of £1,800 for pulling down a venerable and somewhat ramshackle pub where cheap beds were popular with bargemen who worked vessels up to the adjoining wharves of the Medway Navigation Company.

Bartram's replaced the old inn with the present Elizabethan-style Castle Hotel, featuring a landing stage and a terrace overlooking the water.

Replacement of the old bridge constructed a century earlier using some of the materials from even older bridges had become urgent because large piers obstructed the river's flow in time of flood.

The new bridge, built by Wallis and Sons of Maidstone at a cost of £2,146, included handsome cast iron work and gas lanterns (now electrified) by a local foundry, Gray and Sons. Traffic was severely disrupted during the 12 months of construction, but on completion the new Great Bridge was hailed as "an ornament, advantage and improvement to the town".

The townspeople, having endured so much while the work went on, were reluctant to agree to a civic opening. But local pride prevailed and the ceremony took place with members of the Local Board driving up the High Street in a three-horse landau.

Tom Pawley, mine host of the Rose and Crown Hotel, gave a public dinner, and Thomas Vane, grocer and councillor, provided an illuminated barge with vocalists and glee party to entertain crowds on the new bridge and river banks. This was the precursor of the famous Venetian Fetes, highlight of Cricket Week when Kent played on the Angel Ground.

The 1888 builders did their work well, for it was not until 1994 that the Big Bridge had to be substantially strengthened to cope with the enormously increased weight of traffic.

Councillors lead a procession at the opening of the new Great Bridge in 1888. The Castle Hotel (out of view on left) was then a recently opened replacement for the shabby Castle Inn where beggars and tinkers could stay the night for a few pence.

Adam's Ale might be preferred

SOCIETIES devoted to the welfare of travellers, human and animal, set up drinking fountains and troughs at the entrances to towns in the 19th century hoping that thirsty carters would prefer free Adam's Ale to the beer available a few yards away.

A drinking fountain outside the former Star and Garter public house at the junction of London Road and Shipbourne Road was opened in May, 1872. It was designed by architect James Foster Wadmore who lived close by.

Viscount Holmesdale, handily located in Sevenoaks, had agreed to declare the new fountain open but cried off at the last, citing urgent parliamentary business. Perhaps the wet and stormy weather also had something to do with it.

Dr James Welldon, headmaster of Tonbridge School opposite the pub, agreed to deputise. A suitable choice, many thought, because of his rigid puritanical views and readiness to rail against the evils of drink, despite family association with the brewing industry through his mother's name of Ind.

The 14th Kent Rifle Volunteers paraded with their band on a blustery afternoon. Between showers of rain and hail Dr Welldon did all that was hoped of him, ascribing his continuing vigour despite a lifetime's martyrdom to indigestion, to a rigorous regime of Malvern water.

Commending the fountain he said: "Every market day in summer we see most distressing objects in the way of cattle walking footsore and miserable through the town. I won't say that we did not have another object in view, but if this tap turns out a good one it might compete with the tap behind (hear, hear). But it must be a really good one to have an effect in that way.

"If more of this liquor were taken and less of the other we would have happier homes, better fathers, better sons, better husbands and better wives".

Dr and Mrs Welldon, the local MP William Hart-Dyke and other notables drank from the fountain before dashing for shelter, and a cup of tea, in the school.

Despite Dr Welldon's hopes, the Star and Garter flourished as a popular pub for more than a century until, pending demolition for road widening, it was taken over by local churches as a pub with no beer and changed its name to the Star.

At the other end of Tonbridge a drinking fountain placed in the wall of St Stephen's church by Algernon Masters competed with the Imperial opposite (long since gone) for the custom of the chain horse men waiting to help haul heavy loads up Quarry Hill.

This drinking fountain, boldly placed to challenge the Star and Garter pub at the junction of London Road and Shipbourne Road, was opened by Dr James Welldon, headmaster of Tonbridge School, in 1872.

Gracious buildings thrown away

WIDE pavements, elegant lamp standards and traffic-slowing "pinch points" installed above the Big Bridge are a poor substitute for the centuries-old narrow sections that served the same purpose until 1961.

In that year Kent County Council clapped its hands to its ears and dismissed all pleas to save two groups of picturesque buildings, including Angells the jewellers.

My recollection that the former Tonbridge Urban District Council let through this piece of official vandalism almost on the nod was confirmed by Jim Angell, retired head of the family firm.

It was claimed that Angells, and other shops offering an historic frontage similar to the Chequers and its neighbours, had to go because they were in poor condition. This was certainly not so, as two Tonbridge councillors were gracious enough to admit to Mr Angell even before the dust of demolition had settled.

The council reneged on its promise to the Society for the Protection of Ancient Buildings in 1928 to do everything in its power to save the shops. The KCC's determination to have them down — dating from the Great Bridge widening in 1927 — had been condemned as "pointless" by the society's architect Professor Beresford Pile.

The 16th century Angell building was lived in by John Angell and his family until the 1930s. Jim Angell remembered "a bit of plaster flaking from the high front gable, but nothing else was wrong".

Kent County Council bought the old shop and its neighbours for future road widening, keeping the tenants on six months' notice. Then, having applied a tidy planners' solution by pulling down everything from Watergate to the Chequers, the KCC did not know what to do with the vacant land.

A new view of the castle wall was the only benefit. Widening the road when the A21 by-pass was already in the planning stage was soon regretted. The town lost buildings which its people treasured, including the picturesque jumble of Watergate, half a dozen small private shops and Tallyho Alley.

John Angell, who died in 1973, took his shop on a 21-year lease in 1910. He was president of theTonbridge Swimming Club, a Rotarian, Freeman of the City of London and one of that band of High Street traders who managed the local council's affairs so well then.

A row of shops from the former White Hart pub (now Blair House) to Crutch Bros furnishers on the corner of Lansdowne Road made another "pinch point" for which a substitute has had to be found at great expense. The KCC acquired these shops and allowed them to fall into a disgraceful ruin so that they endured too long for the town's good. The planners soon forgot about a proposed new courthouse and a police station on the cleared site and allowed offices instead.

Some of the High Street shops (above) and the We Three Loggerheads pub just below the Big Bridge which were demolished in the council's great High Street clear-up at the turn of the century. Below is John Angell's jeweller's shop in the upper High Street which was destroyed in KCC's 1960s obsession with road widening.

Last days on a busy river

A S recently as 1950 a tug towed a 200-ton barge loaded with coal up the Medway to the gasworks in an effort to revive a trade that once made Tonbridge and Branbridges, East Peckham, thriving ports of the western Weald. It was not a success and the attempt was soon abandoned.

A hundred years earlier most of the barges worked up to Tonbridge were man-hauled. These "hufflers" shared £1 for pulling a barge from Maidstone on ropes attached to their bodies, climbing scores of fences and sometimes plunging chest deep through flood water.

Hufflers often lodged at Wharf Cottages, East Peckham, the home for more than 150 years of the Saunders family. Five generations gathered round the table when David and Alice Saunders celebrated their golden wedding there in the 1930s.

The couple's fathers were barge captains. David Saunders was a mate on the barge *Edward and Martha,* and served 50 years as a water bailiff. He held two Royal Humane Society certificates, having saved six lives. In 1889 he rescued two girls and two boys when their boat capsized. On Boxing Night, 1908, he pulled out two men who walked into the river by the wharf. They belonged to the well-known Jupp family of bargees. Tradition has it that they had sampled too freely from a cargo of Schnapps.

When David Saunders started work, the Medway Barge Company had 18 sailing vessels and 20 lighters working up to Tonbridge. Coal brought from Wales to Rochester in five brigantines was off-loaded into barges for delivery to farms and businesses along the river.

The Medway Navigation Company, founded in 1739, built locks and bridges to make the river navigable up to Tonbridge. It did a lucrative trade carrying iron guns from Sussex and Kent foundries to shipyards on the Thames and monopolised river traffic for more than a century until the railways came.

In 1748 a Heathfield ironmaster, John Fuller, wrote to his London agent: "I send an account of the guns made this year; most of them, I hope, are at the waterside on the Branbridge on the Tonbridge Navigation".

In 1889 barges carried 17,000 pockets (large sacks) of hops to London at half a crown (12p) a pocket. In a price war the rival railway company cut the rate to two shillings, then to 1s 6d. The barge firms could not keep up and lost the hops and other bulk cargoes.

In a last major effort to revive the river trade the two Medway bridges at Branbridges were rebuilt in 1906. It failed and companies using the river, always quarrelsome and locked in interminable litigation, had to accept that their day was done. One by one they collapsed and in 1911 a Conservancy Board took over the river and closed it while neglected locks were rebuilt.

This took several years. By the time the river was usable again the trade had gone for ever.

In recent times the closure of Arnold's (later Arnold and Nathan) riverside works was a further blow, ending a tradition of heavy engineering dating from the construction and repair of steam engines in the 19th century.

New factories have isolated the once thriving riverside community.

Branbridges, often wrongly assumed to be the name of the man who founded the wharves at East Peckham, means bridges made of brands, or planks. The name appears in old documents as Brandtbridge or Brandebrigge, marking an important Medway crossing between London and Wealden country around Paddock Wood.

The streams that vanished

PIPER'S Stream under Tonbridge High Street no longer exists but the site of its former bridge is marked by a plaque recording that it was "repaired at the charge of the countie" in 1628. Many people have been puzzled by this.

Piper's Stream, named after the man who had a business and a chapel beside a little watercourse long since vanished, was one of three small streams under the High Street. The others were the Botany, a considerable and heavily polluted waterway, and Cann's Stream, which ran through the grounds of Bartram's brewery (opposite Woolworth's). All three were filled in or culverted into the main river many years ago.

Only two of the former five High Street bridges (said by some to have given the town its name via Town of Bridges, see p.6) remain, the Great Bridge and Little Bridge, both rebuilt as the town grew. Little Bridge, hump-backed over two spans, was always at risk after heavy rain and succumbed in January, 1814, when a swift thaw following a long frost piled masses of ice against the crumbling brickwork. The bridge gave way, sending a torrent down the street and carrying all before it.

The consequent severe disruption caused the weekly cattle market to be divided into two sections, above and below the broken bridge. Stage coaches and waggons were diverted, some via Postern and others on a long way round through Penshurst and Leigh.

The new bridge lasted until 1871 but was still hump-backed and hardly less convenient than the old one. It had an iron pump on one corner beside Buley's fish shop. The tumbling bay in River Walk, still known as Buley's Weir, had nothing to do with the fishmonger, but his name provided a convenient identification.

Riddle of the Medway cannon

I would be sorry to lay to rest the mystery of the Medway Wharf cannon, which kept Tonbridge chuckling after the Great Bridge was widened amid much pomp and circumstance in 1888. I am confident that I need not do so, despite what I wrote in my Warwick Notebook a century afterwards.

A pair of cannon, presented to the town by the naval authorities at Chatham after Waterloo, marked the borders of the Medway Navigation Company's property and prevented carts cutting the corner as they turned into Medway Wharf Road.

During the bridge rebuilding the Local Board complained that one cannon remaining after road re-alignment obstructed a new footpath and should go, offering £5 compensation. The company's demand for £50 was rejected.

The board had the cannon dug up and dumped it outside the Medway Company's coal store. The company, noted for its arrogance and undisguised contempt for the Local Board, dug it up again, cheered by a gang of sympathisers sensing the makings of a classic Tonbridge row.

The company by a solemn resolution replaced the cannon on the corner, rammed the earth down tight and departed.

Next morning the cannon had gone, apparently spirited away, and no-one really knew what happened to it. One man (unidentified) declared that he would carry the secret to his grave.

At the time local opinion was divided on three theories: that the cannon was consigned to Seale, Austen and Barnes' smelting furnace just round the corner; was pitched over the bridge to vanish in the Medway mud; or was quietly re-possessed by the Medway Company to save face.

Arthur Neve stirred the pot in his *Tonbridge of Yesterday* (1933) by writing:" Without breaking the seal of the confessional, I may state authoritatively that the first and last guesses (that the cannon was melted down, or removed by the Medway Company) are very wide of the mark: the cannon was never melted down and it was not removed by its owners. Further than that I cannot go".

After my article of September, 1988, a reader recalled that two years earlier I had hinted at what he believed was the cannon's true fate: that it was hidden by council officials under the floor of a shed known as the Black Lodge on the Vale Road sewage farm and disinterred secretly and melted down during a scrap metal drive in the second world war.

True or false? The sewage farm manager, the late Fred Harding, was said to be one of the few who knew.

Despite what I have written at various times I think the verdict has to remain: case unproven.

Sailing barges unloading at the Baltic Saw Mills wharf below the Great Bridge.

The Hartlake Bridge tragedy

THERE is a memorial in Hadlow churchyard to 32 victims of the Medway's worst flood disaster. It happened in October 1853 when a waggon loaded with hop-pickers plunged through the grandly-named but perilously rotten Hartlake Bridge between Hadlow and Tudeley.

The bridge, very old with steep approaches on either side, was owned by the Medway Navigation Company which, in its arrogant way, never deigned to notice a disaster waiting to happen.

The day's work in the Hadlow hop gardens over, the pickers were singing merrily as they travelled back to their camps in two waggons. The first carried a heavier load and passed over the bridge safely. As John Waghorne, the driver of the second cart, prepared to cross he asked his 40 passengers to stop singing in case they frightened the horses.

The lead horse was safely over and descending on the Tudeley side when a hoof slipped on an iron plate set into the road to give improved footing.

The traces broke, throwing the second horse off balance. The rear of the waggon swung into the side of the bridge, demolishing the rotten oak slabs and hurling 40 pickers into the swollen river.

Men women and children huddled together in terror in the freezing water. Rescuers arriving quickly from the other cart found many of their friends trapped in the overturned cart. Pitiful cries were heard along the river for more than half an hour but only eight people were saved, one of them a little Irish lad found clinging to a piece of fence.

He had been sitting next to the driver who tried to grab him as the waggon toppled, but he slipped away. The carter jumped sideways and was saved.

Hundreds of shocked people watched in silence as the bodies were recovered the next day. News of the disaster spread rapidly and on the following Sunday crowds went to look at the shattered bridge.

A coroner's jury returned a verdict of accidental death and called on the Medway Navigation Company to build a new bridge. Eventually this was done, although the company never acknowledged the dangerous state of the old one.

It became a custom to throw a wreath into the river from the new bridge during every hop-picking season. Later, for many years, a memorial service was held in Hadlow churchyard and flowers in memory of the 32 who died were placed at the foot of the monument.

The old wooden Hartlake Bridge where 32 hop pickers were drowned in 1853 when a waggon crashed through rotten fencing.

Old pharmacist's remedies live on

HARRY Beckett would be flattered to know that some of the medicines he made famous in his Tonbridge pharmacy at the beginning of the century are still in demand.

Eighty years later his successor at 25 Quarry Hill Road had sufficient regular customers for Beckett's cough remedy and his indigestion mixture to warrant making up a gallon jar of each every two or three weeks, modified slightly to satisfy modern regulations.

The original recipes survive in Beckett's notes of well-tried nostrums for every conceivable ill, though some once-popular remedies can no longer be made: Beckett's special tonic, for instance, which contained the poison strychnine, and his eye drops using morphine.

But his chilblain ointment is still available to sufferers from a painful condition less common now than it was when homes and work places were poorly heated.

Harry Beckett, born in 1861, learned his pharmacy under James Haffenden at Ramsgate and worked as assistant in several London businesses. He developed many other skills but could not realise his main ambition to be a doctor. This did not prevent him acting as ship's doctor on a 76-day journey to Australia in 1884.

Beckett, an accomplished flautist, engineer and photographer, was most celebrated locally as a shilling-a-time tooth puller. Submitting to Harry Beckett's chair was no small act of courage, as Edward Webber, who kept a neighbouring nursery and post office, recalled.

"He had an ancient armchair the arms of which one was instructed to grip tightly and not let go," said Mr Webber.

"This was a great test of fortitude and the ensuing tug of war, without anaesthetics, still produces painful memories."

Routine dispensing tried Beckett's patience. Customers calling him away from his preferred photographic and engineering work in the back room would feel the sting of his sharp tongue.

His forthright opinions on almost any topic usually ran contrary to the prevailing view. He was contemptuous of authority and when swimming with friends up the river always hung his clothes on a "Bathing strictly prohibited" sign, on the back of which he recorded the date and water temperature.

The Becketts were a talented family. A brother pioneered the use of X-ray machines in Australia, and tragically lost both hands in an experiment. Another brother made industrial diamonds, and Harry Beckett's son Tom was an accomplished cabinet maker.

Harry Beckett was a smart dresser, favouring in summer narrow white flannelette trousers creased at the sides and a white panama hat with a bright band which he re-painted each season.

Ingredients for his medicines were delivered in bulk and mixed by Beckett in his dispensary. Bottles containing a murky residue of the original potions survived in dark corners of the shop's basement. Beckett told a friend that his best seller was a digestive mixture made from peppermint and distilled water.

Ernest Upton was trained by Beckett from 1903 and eventually took over the business, moving it from 3 Quarry Hill Road (which used to be called Priory Terrace) to No 25 in 1934. He, too, had many skills, ranging from "putting down" domestic pets by gassing in a sealed chamber, to dispensing spectacles, using simple eye-testing equipment and a range of lenses.

Sidney Brown joined the business and it traded as Upton and Brown until Mr Upton died in 1949.

In modernising the shop the present owner David Poile had to part with much of Beckett's equipment, including his pill rolling machine and a fearsome set of dental instruments.

The old notebooks will never be destroyed. In them Beckett's "Stand easy" foot powder and his corn and wart solvent (1905) are sandwiched between guidance on wiping a joint, French polishing, mixing green paint and whitewash ("for shop walls") and Beckett's recipe for straw hat cleaning. The hat had to be left to dry in a cool cellar for 24 hours, then smoothed with a warm flat iron.

Scores of letters in their original envelopes disprove — in Harry Beckett's case at least — the popular suspicion that these unsolicited testimonials for medical remedies owed most to the advertiser's imagination.

From Eton College in 1905, E. Johnson wrote: "I have received the mixture quite safe and have recommended it to all my friends".

A letter (1926, when a film for developing went astray) addressed to "The nearest chemist on the left side of Tonbridge station" would still find Harry Beckett's former shop.

When the clock mender called

CLOCK repairing in the days when every home had a wind-up timepiece was a skill practised by itinerant experts. The Lockyer brothers, Charlie and Albert, who had a business in East Street, Tonbridge, used to walk round a circuit of villages, visiting each about once a fortnight doing on-the-spot repairs or collecting faulty clocks and returning them on the next call.

People needing the brothers' services would leave word at the local pub or shop. Their shop was alive with the ticking of clocks, punctuated by the chiming of full hours, halves and quarters, sometimes lasting several minutes before a customer could be attended to.

Mr Nice the paraffin man

FREDERICK Nice was known to hundreds of people in Tonbridge and district through his extensive business selling paraffin, hardware and groceries, first from a horse-drawn van, then a Model-T Ford and other vehicles.

He brought up his family of seven after his wife died in childbirth and worked in his Domestic Oil Stores in Barden Road until a few months before his death in 1959 at the age of 92.

He was assisted in the shop by his daughter Gertrude and on the van by her sister Irene, who wore a beret to protect her hair which she plaited in elaborate "earphones".

The other children were Trissie, Eva, Jock, Fred and Connie (Mrs Omer) who at the time of writing was in her eighties and the sole survivor, living in sheltered accommodation.

Old Mr Nice was recalled with affection by his grand-daughter Mrs Eileen Bramley (daughter of Jock), who sometimes helped her grandad on the van and sympathised with customers' complaints that the groceries tasted of paraffin. On Saturdays she earned sixpence in the shop weighing out currants and sultanas into blue bags.

Fred Nice graduated to motor transport after years with a horse and cart. On his first excursion behind the wheel in Tonbridge High Street he nearly had an accident through shouting "Whoa" instead of stamping on the brake.

Father and daughter made regular deliveries of paraffin and methylated spirit in Tonbridge and the villages around. The shop was a fascinating emporium of household equipment such as brooms and brushes, washing bowls and buckets, clothes lines, rope, string and wire, pegs and blue bags, lamp wicks, hearth stone, gas mantles and fly papers.

Frank Head, who grew up in Lower Hayesden, remembered Mr Nice calling with paraffin and groceries every Monday. "We always had custard creams as a treat and enjoyed them despite the taste of paraffin".

Barden Road was one of Tonbridge's busiest streets in Mr Nice's time. His neighbours included a baker, where cakes, sold fresh daily, could be obtained cheaply the day after, the Southern Stores (on the station side) and Froud's dairy, where milk was dispensed from brass churns in the cool tiled shop.

The Redcar garage went through from Barden Road to Avebury Avenue and horse cabs waited for fares at the near entrance to the station beside the parcels office.

Frederick Nice and friends out with his horse and cart at flood time in Barden Road. A painting made from a snapshot.

An old-time ironmonger

IN selecting an old-time business typical of so many in Tonbridge early this century my choice fell on Woodmans the ironmongers with its staff who knew the name of everything and where to find it.

If the tiers of drawers could not supply a customer's need, he might be conducted on a journey of identification to mysterious regions in the cellar or upstairs.

Rarely was an old-time ironmonger such as Woodmans, Whites or Hutchinson Roe defeated. You could buy one screw or a gross. Nothing came in those plastic packs containing just one fewer or three more than required.

Woodmans, 133 High Street, Tonbridge, a few doors above the Rose and Crown, was run by three generations of the Woodman family until being taken over by White's, another local business whose premises near the Chequers fell to the KCC's enthusiasm for road widening.

Woodmans dated from Victorian times when Frank Woodman acquired the business from Humphrey Wightwick in whose tallow chandlery he started as a boy. When Frank Woodman retired in 1906 the shop passed to his son, Frank Thomas, and within memory was known as F.T.Woodman and Son.

Like most "real" ironmongers, Woodmans also mixed paint. Factory-filled tins in standard colours were unknown. The shop was packed to the doors with goods of every description. Pails and kettles hung from the ceiling. There were copper moulds, fire guards, steel fenders, fly papers, rolling pins and flat irons, overalls and pinafores, paraffin lamps and gas mantles. Displays overflowed on to the pavement.

In the 19th century some of the merchandise for Woodmans and other shops arrived by barge at the wharf beside the Great Bridge.

Leslie Woodman, the last of his family in the business, retired in 1960 after more than 50 years behind the counter. The shop found a new owner and continued to prosper until it succumbed to pressure from the DIY super stores. It is now a restaurant.

L.F.Woodman (right) with his staff in 1960.

The Domestic Bazaar in the High Street supplied everything for the home at keen prices.

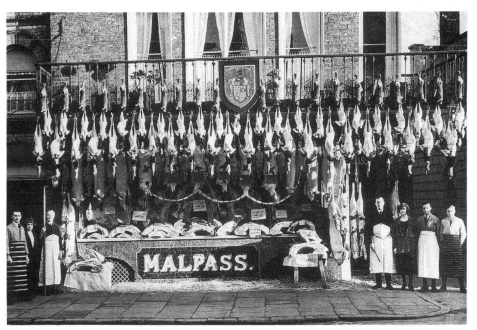

The Malpass family's shop on the corner of Church Lane dressed for Christmas

The haberdasher banker

THOMAS Beeching succeeded as a banker in Tonbridge after a partnership of rich men failed because farmers knew their money was safe with a trusted linen draper.

No pictures of Thomas survive, but family tradition recalls him as a severe looking man with grey side whiskers and a gold watch chain. He was born in 1767 and "from boyhood seems to have possessed the faculty of thinking for himself", according to local historian Arthur Neve.

After gaining financial experience in London, Thomas Beeching arrived in Tonbridge in 1789 and opened a large linen draper's shop on the corner of Church Lane and High Street.

Success came swiftly through the good relations he established with local shopkeepers. Soon they and their customers, mainly farmers coming to market, realised that their money was safer under Beeching the haberdasher's counter than under the mattress at home. Little traders dependent for their incomes on the seasons, particularly hop-picking, turned to Thomas Beeching for help. Soon banking overtook the linen drapery side.

Thomas Beeching's three sons, Horatio, Stephen and Arthur Thomas, all joined the business, living with their parents on the bank's premises. They worked hard, invested wisely and lent prudently to avoid the pitfalls which brought down the Tonbridge Bank and ruined its once-wealthy partners, George Children and William Woodgate, in 1812.

Beeching gave his draper's shop a facelift in 1814 and went over entirely to banking. The following year he issued his own banknotes.

Horatio Beeching (1798-1879), who took over the business at a time when small banks were failing everywhere, was as wise as his father. Beechings weathered the storms to receive in 1826 a commendation from leading citizens of Tonbridge expressing "entire confidence in the safety and responsibility of the Bank of Messrs Beeching and Son and declare their readiness to receive their notes...".

The signatories included J.E.West, of Tonbridge Castle, Thomas Knox, headmaster of Tonbridge School, William Jewhurst, of the Town Mills, John Carnell and John Scoones, solicitors, Sir Charles Hardinge, Vicar of Tonbridge, and John Evenden, chemist.

Horatio was strong in the arm as well as the head. In 1857, surprising three desperadoes about to rob his bank, he set about them with his stick to such effect that they fled, abandoning boots, hat, cap and the drill they had ready to force the door.

Beechings soon opened a branch in Tunbridge Wells, contributing one of the town's finest buildings on the corner of Crescent Road and Mount Pleasant.

Horatio and his family prospered, buying Ferox Hall at Tonbridge

— former home of the failed banker Children — and the adjoining Bordyke Estate of 14 acres. When Mr Beeching married again after being left a widower, he moved to Tunbridge Wells, to please his new bride.

There in the handsome Bank House attached to the office, valued customers were entertained to port and sherry in the parlour before broaching the vulgar subject of money.

The Tonbridge connection was not ignored and, some years after his marriage, Arthur Thomas moved into Ferox Hall, at that time a handsome old house in which Queen Elizabeth had slept on one of her many progresses through Kent. The house was substantially altered in 1880, and eventually sold to Tonbridge School.

The pride of the Beechings suffered a serious blow in the 1880s when a partner, Mr W.Hodgkin, speculated rashly on the Stock Exchange and ruined the bank. Debts of some £100,000 had to be repaid, and Beechings sold out to Lloyds for a figure said to represent four years' profits.

Lloyds' confidence in the Beeching integrity was unshaken, however, and they retained several members of the family as managers.

Two Miss Beechings lived in Bordyke for many years and worked hard for Tonbridge Parish Church, especially with young people.

Cobbling among the cobwebs

TAKING one's shoes to the "snob" was a familiar errand years ago when Tonbridge had at least a dozen shoe repairers practising their craft in tiny workshops.

One of the oldest was in Waterloo Road, last owned by John Moon whose small stature fitted him perfectly for the ancient building's 6ft high rooms.

He took over the centuries-old shop beside the former Good Intent pub in 1959 when his employer Arthur Gurr retired. For six-footer Mr Gurr and his equally tall predecessor, Alf Ollerenshaw, the brick-floored one-time beerhouse was always a tight fit and they became stooped with the passing years.

Mr Ollerenshaw lived in Leigh and played centre forward for the village football team. He travelled to Tonbridge each day by train carrying a sack full of boots and shoes for repair.

He took over the shop from Mr Cash, and was the last to follow a century-old tradition of each new owner paying part of the profits to the widow of his predecessor.

The cobbler's shop was pulled down in 1971. Thought to date from Tudor times, it would have been one of the few buildings in the grounds of the former Tonbridge Priory.

Coming of the railway

TONBRIDGE might never have been an important railway junction if Maidstone had not set its mind against the Iron Road in mid-Victorian times. The result to this day is that Kent's county town is nothing in railway terms.

Notices of proposed new lines came up every few years. As early as 1825 the Tunbridge Wells and Maidstone Railway Company held a general meeting of proprietors and supporters at the Sussex Hotel, Tunbridge Wells, to hear reports of the Engine and Provisional Committee.

Estimated costings for several routes to Maidstone and Snodland, also an Edenbridge branch, were presented by John Stone, the company's secretary and solicitor.

These local entrepreneurs made no further progress and eventually joined an amalgamation which made Tonbridge a main railway centre in 1842. Anti-railway Maidstone got no second chance, leaving Tonbridge to be developed even before a direct line to London via Sevenoaks in 1868 made it the junction of four routes.

From 1842 to 1868 Tonbridge station was on the site of the later goods yard between Vale Road and Priory Road and trains ran to London via Redhill. When the station moved to the present location the old road to Tunbridge Wells via the present Barden Road and Waterloo Road had to be cut and a new main road constructed from the Angel (Vale Road-High Street junction) to the foot of Quarry Hill at Brook Street..

A former farm lane became Vale Road and Priory Road was built from the new Tunbridge Wells road to Strawberry Vale. Houses soon filled a new complex of residential roads off another new main route to Hastings, Pembury Road.

For many years until it got its own church, St Stephen's, old Tonbridge was suspicious of this so-called New Town. The prospect of a journey over the Station Arch, past Rogues Hole where rail-borne criminals gathered and into a dimly-lit region of muddy lanes alarmed the timid.

Long after the new station opened to serve the line to London via Sevenoaks the stiff climb out of Tonbridge towards Tunbridge Wells taxed the early locomotives. Trains backed out of Tonbridge on to a loop near Hectorage Road to reduce the gradient before tackling the steepest part.

Tonbridge historian Arthur Neve never travelled in the roofless carriages of the early days, but wrote: "I have often ridden in a third class carriage open from end to end, and constructed with as many angles and as few curves as possible, in which the seat was bare board, which had no luggage rack and no heating, and in which microscopic windows were set so high as, even when clean, to be almost useless for seeing the country".

Territorial Sunday in Tonbridge in 1914 showing the railway signals building opposite the station. It was destroyed by fire a few years later, depriving Tonbridge of its only reliable public clock.

Brown's newsagents and barber shop in Shipbourne Road. The newspaper posters suggest a date just before the 1914-18 war.

Mr H.W. Davis was a familiar figure in the 1920s flying down Castle Hill with cut wood piled on his home-made wooden trike. He was also a skilled wine maker. He would entertain friends on a Sunday morning to sample potent brews matured in old rum casks. In winter he breakfasted on broth made with elderberry wine to keep out the cold while he worked in the woods. He could not read or write but calculated accurately by a system he called "pot hooks and hangers".

Florrie Race, known as 'Puss', was an early motorcyclist and one of the daughters of Isaac Race, auctioneer and leading townsman.

Our old monks rest under the railway

LINES for a new railway took precedence over the remains of Tonbridge Priory of St Mary Magdalene in 1842. Few gave thought to the generations of old monks in their stone coffins being tumbled into the foundations of the railway yard between Vale Road and Priory Road.

There had been a flurry of interest some twenty years earlier when men digging for stones in the priory ruins found a coffin shaped to the head and feet containing a body bound in a waxed cloth.

James Phippen, who edited Colbran's *Tunbridge Wells Guide* wrote: "Part of the cloth being removed, the body presented an appearance somewhat like dried clay, the larger muscles retaining their form, but upon the touch of the workmen mouldered into dust".

Close by was a skeleton and the iron bands and nails of its wooden coffin. The men also found a stone coffin close to the surface, a sculptured coffin-shaped stone, and a skeleton with its head resting on a tile.

At this stage the Rev Thomas Knox, headmaster of Tonbridge School, intervened and further excavation was stopped. One of the coffins was acquired by James Alexander and placed in the garden of his Somerhill mansion, where it is still.

The other relics, and a skeleton found in 1934 when a new signal box was built, were lost, probably when the short-lived Tonbridge museum was abandoned.

A pity, for the story of St Mary Magdalene and its Black Canons is a romantic one.

When Richard de Clare of Tonbridge Castle arrived to lay the priory foundation stone in about 1124 a Thomas Geoffrey was on the verge of being executed for theft. His life was saved by de Clare's declaration that "it is not fitting that such a gift should be baptised with an evil-doer's blood".

Geoffrey's good luck cancelled out an earlier misfortune when he and John Wrancke, who was also suspected of the theft, were ordered to fight, the loser to face the charge. Wrancke won and went free.

The priory's foundation was commemorated by a Tonbridge schoolchildren's pageant in the Castle Grounds in 1909. The boy playing the prior was given these words to say of de Clare's act of mercy: "We would beg that as forgiven sin this stone anoints, so shall our house be named the priory of St Mary Magdalene".

It was said to be the burial place of another Richard de Clare, who owned Tonbridge Castle in the reign of Henry VIII.

The priory was one of 40 small monasteries dissolved and sold by Cardinal Wolsey under an order obtained from Rome in 1523. The money helped to build Cardinal College, Oxford.

The extensive priory lands were part of the lowy of Tonbridge given to de Clare by William the Conqueror's son Rufus. It had income from rents, including the right to graze 120 hogs in the Tonbridge forests, the gift of two loads of wood daily and one buck on the Feast of St Mary Magdalene.

From their consistory, chapter house, dormitory, refectory, vestry and library the Black Canons went out preaching. Monks who helped rebuild the priory after a fire in 1337 were awarded an indulgence of 40 days, plus a range of spiritual blessings. They lived well: food for Christmas Day in the reign of Edward I included 200 loaves, two hams, two pigs, two quarters of beef, six cocks, one boar, mustard, wine, 100 herrings, two and a half casks of ale and one of better beer.

The Cardinal's Error pub takes its name from Wolsey's failure to achieve his promise to provide Tonbridge with a free grammar school with places for 40 pupils in exchange for the priory. When he consulted the "principal inhabitants" as directed, they asked to retain the priory "if it might stand with the King's pleasure". Wolsey was nonplussed. While he cogitated, the priory was closed and he fell from favour. So Tonbridge got nothing and had to wait for Sir Andrew Judde to found the free grammar school in 1553.

George Mackley's drawing showing the last days of the Priory of St Mary Magdalene which stood between Vale Road and Priory Road. The ruins, and the coffins of the old Black Canons who went out preaching from the priory were unceremoniously tipped into the foundations of the new railway in 1842.

Steam enthusiast

JACK Roper, who died aged 80 in 1984, was a bank manager by day, but in the evenings and week-ends for fifty years he was out with his camera recording the steam railways of this area.

Two nieces to whom he was a much-loved and ever fascinating uncle ignored an instruction to his executors to destroy his collection of photographs and negatives.

Remembering long waits on Devil's Bridge, Postern Lane, Tonbridge, while their uncle photographed the passage of an important train, they ensured that his lifetime's work was passed to railway museums and collectors.

Jack Roper married Isabel Race, one of the nine daughters of Isaac Race, Tonbridge auctioneer and estate agent, a JP and a local councillor who was largely responsible for the town's decision to build its own electricity generating station.

Although they had no children, Jack and Isabel Roper were a popular uncle and aunt, widely travelled and always interesting company. Jack's hobbies embracing photography, painting, meteorology and the construction of huge box kites "got almost out of hand at times" according to a niece. But his company was always stimulating.

Jack Roper and his brothers went to Tonbridge School. He had a weak heart as a boy and spent some years in a spinal carriage. He was never really strong, but in his last year declared with pride, "You see, I've made it to eighty".

His meticulously labelled collection of hundreds of prints and glass slides, of windmills, watermills and buildings as well as railways live on in various collections and museums.

Cool heads prevented a rail tragedy

TWO railwaymen kept their heads and averted a major disaster when a boat train and a local train collided at Tonbridge station on March 5, 1909. The crash, in which two men died, was well recorded on souvenir postcards.

It was said that a railway official's attempts to make a train from Tonbridge to Redhill travel faster than was prudent caused the driver to miss a signal warning of an oncoming train on another line.

The 9am boat train from Charing Cross to Dover was rounding the main line curve just outside the station when the Redhill train crossed in front. The boat train's engine hit the tender of the local train, smashing a fish van and scattering its load on the snow-covered track.

The only good thing to come out of the accident was a plentiful supply of fish for people who scrambled over fences from adjoining houses.

The Redhill train's fireman Henry Howard and loco inspector R. L. Rowley, who was riding in the cab and allegedly urged Howard to go too fast, were killed.

A second and potentially more disastrous crash was averted by a ticket inspector, Mr Agnew, waving a warning to an approaching express from Margate. Another inspector, Mr Harvey, threw his cap at the driver. This train stopped only 150 yards from the wreckage.

Forty minutes later the Royal train carrying King Edward VII and Queen Alexandra was due at Tonbridge. A warning was telegraphed up the line and the train was stopped at Orpington and shunted on to a loop line to get the King and Queen to Dover via Chatham.

As a result of the accident a sharp bend in the London line was recognised as a hazard and opened out.

A wrecked locomotive in a crash that killed two men at Tonbridge station in 1909.

The puritan prude who didn't mind a bit

GIRLS in micro monokinis as seen on today's holiday beaches would have been beyond the imagination of Donald Clark, a Tonbridge councillor whose opposition to mixed bathing in 1920 made him a national figure celebrated in the music halls as "The Puritan Prude".

It all began innocently enough with Tonbridge Swimming Club's request for men and women to be allowed to swim together in the town pool from 6am till 10am on Sundays, thus breaching the council's rule keeping the sexes apart.

The call to refuse the swimming club's application came from another councillor, but it was Donald Clark's speech that caught the attention of Arthur Doody, editor of the *Tonbridge Free Press*. He knew a good story when he saw it and set Clark on the way to unsought fame.

This former Scots Guards officer, who served in the relief of General Gordon in 1881 and was decorated for bravery and twice mentioned in despatches in the Boer War, was an unlikely candidate for the title of Britain's Mixed Bathing Censor.

He won headlines in a news-starved summer by declaring that he spoke his mind "not because I am a Puritan but in the interests of ladies looking for husbands".

He added that more potential partners had been lost on the beaches of Brighton than anywhere else, the result of a young man's shock on seeing his pretty dance partner of the night before looking ridiculous in a scanty bathing costume "with her hair drawn up under a horrible rubber hat".

Arthur Doody alerted the *Daily Mail* to this ideal Silly Season story. The paper engaged Donald Clark, sometimes accompanied by Doody, to tour English seaside resorts from Margate to the Isle of Wight in search of "proper women's swimming wear".

Clark, then aged 62, found little to please him, and delighted his sponsors by declaring that from what he had seen, strict government supervision should be applied to bathing places. In his view mixed bathing "must always have a debasing influence by lowering the respect that should obtain between the sexes".

When the story died with the end of the outdoor swimming season in September the censorious Clark was taken up by the music halls and featured in pantomime as "The Puritan Prude who was Horribly Rude".

They were really too late, for Tonbridge Swimming Club's application had been approved by the urban district council by ten votes to six and the sexes swam together for the first time on a Sunday morning in July, 1920.

The club made it a gala occasion by inviting swimmers from all over Kent, including Mrs Hilda Wilding, the Medway ladies champion who was about to make an attempt on the English Channel. Donald Clark stayed away, but the Press were there in force to hear Mrs Wilding's cautious view that while mixed swimming should be encouraged, men and women "should keep to their respective sides of the bath".

When the permitted session from 6am till 10am was over, a merry party of bathers and Press sought out Donald Clark at his home Hill Crest, Hildenborough, and received a convivial welcome. He declined Mrs Wilding's invitation to withdraw his remark that women bathers' caps made them look "like Skye terriers".

Clark, who died aged 70 in 1928, never shrank from controversy and served Tonbridge with distinction. He was popular with ex-servicemen of the Great War for pleading at the age of 57 to be allowed to fight in France with the Royal West Kent Regiment.

Rejected as too old, he served by training young men for the new armies. His election as chairman of the council in 1918 gave him the honour of presenting the town's certificates of appreciation to returning servicemen.

Tonbridge municipal swimming pool in the 1950s. Built in 1910, it remained popular as an outdoor heated pool until 1993 when it was closed to be replaced by a new indoor-outdoor facility. (This was nearing completion at the time of writing.)

Venetian Fete was Tonbridge's pride

VENETIAN fetes in Tonbridge between the wars, and for the three years of their revival in the 1950s, were the town's premier outdoor social event.

Before the Angel Ground was damaged beyond further use as a county ground in the second world war, the colourful parade of decorated boats was always held in Cricket Week.

Thousands lined the river to watch beautiful craft glide beneath the castle walls to the judges' stand at Watergate.

Programmes for Venetian fetes sixty and seventy years ago capture the flavour of this marvellous event. In 1933, for instance, the festivities began with a diving display (fancy diving into the murky Medway now!) and crowds waiting for darkness to fall cheered the exertions of the ladies' canoe races.

The line-up was Miss Eileen Ives and Miss Dorothy Hall v Miss Phyllis Paynter and Miss Joan Merry, Miss Gladys Burr and Miss Joan Mackley v Miss Watson and Miss Franklin, Miss Mildred Cope and Miss Enid Cox v Mrs Houston and Mrs Healey, Miss Madge Dugdale and Miss Janet Pettijohn v Miss Pauline Daniel and Miss Kinross. Most of these ladies paddled highly varnished and gold-lettered craft belonging to the exclusive Tonbridge Boating Club. Sir Robert Jackson was starter.

The Procession of Illuminated Craft, starting with the explosion of a maroon, was divided into three classes: decorated boats or punts with historical or artistic tableaux entered by clubs or associations; similar private entries; canoes; advertisements and miscellaneous.

The 3rd Tonbridge (Corpus Christi) Rover crew put in HMS Nelson. The 1st Tonbridge Boys Brigade had Vive le Sport: 'Not for the sake of ribboned coat, Or the selfish help of season's fame, But his captain's hand on his shoulder smote: 'Play up! Play up! and Play the game!'

Tunbridge Wells youth branch of the League of Nations Union chose a serious theme, Japanese Diplomacy, while the unemployed of the town's Excelsior Club presented their view of The Dole. Tonbridge Amateur Dramatic Society did Hey Diddle Diddle, with cat, fiddle and a cow jumping over the moon. The 1st Tonbridge Rover Scouts presented a home version of the Chicago gangsters in Bumped Off.

Individual entries, often the most colourful, included M.S.B.Reeves' Golden Gondola, Charles Batchelor's Camping, John Wotherspoon's The Origin, Rosamund Mabey's Lament for Icarus, Sydney Norton's Venetian Gondola and Charles Barkaway, Ken Baker and Rupert Steed with a combined entry called Willowby

Miss Dora Reed's Cinderella's Slipper was the only entry in the canoe class.

In the advertisement section F C Couchman had The Magic Carpet and Miss G Miller advocated Pure Drugs.

Over the years most boats graduated from candle lights to battery power, although it was generally agreed that the old style was best. Rupert Steed, of the Local Amateur Musical Players, solved the problem of lighting in a wind by projecting a flame from a tube.

Tonbridge police took part in 1928 with Hot Dinner in the Solomon Islands — a theme certain to attract charges of racism today. The British Legion usually chose something solemn recalling the dead of the first world war: Poppies in 1928 and Menin Gate the following year. Mrs Ruth Knowles, of Ramhurst Manor, Leigh, entered The Friend Ship on behalf of her international youth club.

Why did Tonbridge abandon its Venetian Fete, which was without doubt the town's most popular event? There are a number of reasons.

First, the difficulty of finding a group willing and able to supply the level of organisation needed; second, the demise of the old-time boat houses and non-replacement of punts, which were the best craft for mounting a tableau; third, persuading people and organisations to devote weeks creating an entry; fourth, the loss of privately-owned large businesses able to spare time and resources to prepare a boat.

Older members of LAMPS recall the investment of effort needed to achieve a design of which they could be proud. The society's team prefabricated their entry to fit the chosen boat and mounted it a few hours before the fete.

The Venetian Fete was a success story of more leisured times. Everyone loved it and there was little risk of the hooliganism which would threaten a revived parade of delicately balanced craft today. I would like to see the Venetian Fete restored, but I fear there is no chance.

Firemen entered this dramatic tableau in the Venetian Fete of 1952.

Going to the pictures

TONBRIDGE has no cinema now, but between the wars when "going to the pictures" was a weekly treat it offered a choice of four.

Before the challenge of the sumptuous Ritz in Botany in 1935, the Pavilion in Avebury Avenue, converted by our leading entrepreneur Buster West from a former corn store, was regarded as marginally superior to the Capitol, built in 1874 as the Public Hall. The ex-farm buildings of the Star in Bradford Street, offering minimal comfort and always at risk from winter floods, came a poor third.

But Star patrons could admire the skill of its pianist Miss Skinner reading her newspaper while playing a tune to match the action in a silent film.

On stormy nights the staff checked the river level before deciding whether to take out the seats and the piano, or trust to luck and go home. If they got it wrong the seats had to be carried to the electricity works and dried on top of the furnace.

Everything changed with the opening of the Ritz, a luxurious cavern of deep carpets, velvet seats, gilded plaster and super loos, plus a restaurant with music and dancing. The Star closed and the Pavilion and Capitol felt dowdy.

Tonbridge's first films were shown early in the century in the Central Hall, part of a former chapel beside the Little Bridge.

For the young in the twenties and thirties there was the Bug Hutch, otherwise the Empire Theatre in Avebury Avenue where Buster West presided over a Saturday morning menu of cowboy tales and startling thrillers.

Wearing his bowler hat and a fierce expression, he took the money and struggled to impose order on an unruly mob for whom a small extra charge to occupy the gallery included the unspoken right to bombard the stalls with apple cores, and worse.

The Empire was re-named the Repertory Theatre, home of the popular County Players. After the war, as The Playhouse, it became run-down and cheerless. It was demolished in 1968.

Phil Mandel's Riverside Cafe, built entirely of corrugated iron and smelling of cats, The Rink with a concert party and reputedly one of the best roller skating floors for miles around, Doust's boathouse, and a reconstituted former army canteen called the Medway Hall made Bradford Street a main centre of entertainment in the first half of the twentieth century.

All have gone, replaced by offices, supermarkets and car parks.

The Public Hall (later to become the Capitol) opened as a cinema in 1921 with Mary Pickford in Suds. *Washing in a real tub was part of the promotion.*

Great days at the Old Barn

THE Old Barn in Stocks Green Road, Hildenborough, the area's premier social venue between the wars, grew out of a tea room started by chance after Commander Arthur Tomlinson took pity on a hungry film crew who knocked at his door.

He had his cook feed them on eggs, new bread, cream, honey and all the best of farm fare. Of course they told their friends who told other friends. Soon the Old Barn with its huge sign promising "Oceans of Cream" was pulling in passing drivers, bikers and hikers, and black tie parties in the evening.

Between the wars the enterprising, if slightly eccentric, Commander added a swimming pool, a menagerie, marvellous gardens and a Tower of Babel into which revellers could cement their own bottles.

Much of this was destroyed in wartime occupation, but with peace and the end of petrol rationing the Barn became as popular as ever. Reginald and Sheila Tomlinson took over after their father died in 1959, but in 1990, after the deaths within a few days of Sheila and his brother Arthur, Reginald felt he could not carry on alone and posted a sad notice: "Closed for end of season. The last tea with oceans of cream has been served."

Friends tried to persuade Reg Tomlinson to start again, but the spirit had gone and he died in 1994.

The tea room and the great barn where hundreds danced on many a New Year's Eve became marooned in the long nineties' recession until new owners brought the place to life — not without controversy due to the youth and exuberance of its weekend clientele.

In the old days dancing in the great barn on a winter's night could be something of an ordeal. Coke braziers dotted about heated only the area immediately around and dancers had to rely mainly on their own energy to keep warm. Conditions were less spartan after the Tomlinsons installed centralised warm air heating, though many regular clients claimed they missed the braziers.

In Commander Tomlinson's time the Old Barn prospered because he never missed an opportunity for publicity. He had a small airfield, imported a windmill, set up a pottery, made his own bricks, owned a fire engine, put up stocks and had yokels sitting in them, and sold coal brought up river in his motor barge the Saucy Kipper. He advertised that his coal "contained just as many brickbats, slate, slack and dust " as any other, but was a penny a hundredweight cheaper.

He paraded attractive animals from his zoo to catch the passing trade and dressed Ted Morley, a retired Tonbridge horse cabman, in a gorgeous uniform to handle the car parking.

The Old Barn went on war service from the first days of September, 1939. Young Reginald came home from school to find his father recalled to the navy and the staff standing by to receive evacuee children in the care of 19 nurses. They never arrived. Instead the Old Barn became a hostel for workers at Johnson and Jorgensen's glass works evacuated to Frank Woolley's indoor cricket school just up the road.

In later use as an emergency food store it came close to collapse when the ancient walls bulged under pressure from hundreds of tons of sugar and corned beef piled on the dance floor. It was several years before the old timbers resumed their normal places.

Despite severe damage caused by several periods of army occupation, the Barn got going again to relieve the austerities of post-war domestic rationing. But the Tower of Babel, the menagerie, the stocks, the swimming pool and much else that made the Old Barn famous had gone for ever. It was never quite the same.

A Tower of Babel constructed from discarded bottles was a feature of the Old Barn, Hildenborough. Guests were supplied with cement to add their own bottles to the collection.

Jack's proud car came a cropper

THE site of the former Town Mills in Cannon Lane, Tonbridge, now entirely covered by DIY super centres, might have become a rival to Dagenham if the Storey car company had fulfilled its owner's dreams in 1920-21.

It announced a range of cars far too ambitious for its resources, including the sturdy four-seater Tonbridge Saloon and a two-seater coupé. Both bore the distinctive oval radiator desribed as "a sign of the excellence so typical of every Storey model".

The Tonbridge Saloon with a 20 horse power French engine and Daimler transmission cost £1200.

Jack Storey got three production bays going at Town Mills, but the business never caught up with the promise of his advertising.

The fate of the first car off the line might have hinted at what was to come. It was due to be driven along the assembly track by the chief tester Arthur Savage, whose father was landlord of the Half Moon inn at Hildenborough. But the assembly foreman, bursting with pride in the car he had made, became so excited that he leaped behind the wheel and ran it off the track, pushing back the radiator.

Storey, furious, and embarrassed before his invited guests, had the car manhandled back on the track and the radiator was propped up for Bert Flemons, recorder of so many great Tonbridge moments, to take the official photograph.

Storey sold only a few cars and he went bankrupt in 1931 leaving a legacy of disgruntled workers who had given up safe jobs with other employers for the newcomer's short-lived high wages.

Car mass production evolved elsewhere, and Jack Storey and his Tonbridge Saloon are recalled now only as minor footnotes in motoring history.

Tonbridge had other car makers, albeit on a much less ambitious level than Jack Storey. One of them, Herbert Ellis Hall, who had a business in the High Street, opposite Botany, borrowed the registration number KN1 from his son's Flutterby motorcycle and assigned it to his hand-built 20hp Talbot-based landaulette.

Despite his claim that it was "sweet running" and covered 40,000 trouble-free miles, in 1919 it remained a one-off oddity.

I heard in 1990 that it had been rescued — less its valuable number plate — and was being restored by a Dutch enthusiast.

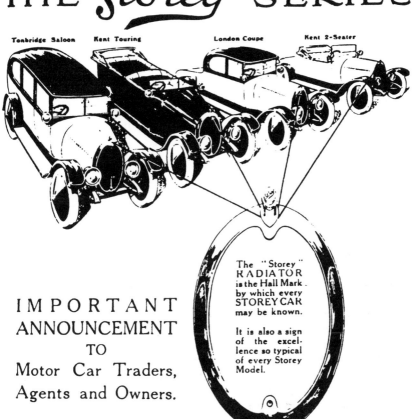
*An oval radiator distinguished Jack Storey's range of cars made at Town Mills,
Tonbridge, after the Great War.*

Ball workers liked a "snob day" off

WHEN cricket ball making was an important Tonbridge industry skilled craftsmen moved between half a dozen small workshops to sustain an income in this notoriously unstable employment. They were also sturdily independent, taking a "snob day" off for drinking and merrymaking when the spirit moved them.

Most worked at some time in the Duke family's factory at Chiddingstone Causeway founded by Timothy Duke, a farmer whose first proper cricket ball in 1760 replaced the home-made ball of leather thongs bound on a hard core.

The journeymen ball makers, often former saddlers or bootmakers, tried to organise themselves in 1897 by forming the Amalgamated Society of Cricket Ball Makers with a registered office at the Mitre Hotel in Hadlow Road, Tonbridge. But they were invariably out-manoeuvered by the employers.

By 1907 the golden age of English ball-making was over and there were only 186 members, 56 having been struck off for being in arrears with subscriptions. Work was slack and many craftsmen were without jobs.

But their spirit never failed. In 1913 Tonbridge ballmakers marching behind a band to Penshurst failed to persuade the Duke's men to join them in a dispute and settled for a day's drinking instead.

The owners had their Cricket Ball Manufacturers' Association, and in 1923 added the prefix English to mark disapproval of increasing competition from Australian and Indian machine-made balls. All the local firms such as Dukes, Ives, Lillywhites, Wisdens, Surridge, Hitchcocks (at Hildenborough), Readers (Teston) and Tworts were members.

The Tonbridge workers made a bid for such profits as there were by setting up a "commune" workshop in an old skating rink in Bradford Street. A few worked there full time but most did extra early or late shifts, sharing the proceeds from the balls they made. Tom Ives, who had a ball factory in Barden, was furious, particularly because he suspected the workshop of providing cut price balls to Gamages, a big London store.

Inevitably the enterprise failed. The men returned to the established workshops and continued the tactic of quitting their benches and demanding a pay rise when their product was in most demand.

Most of the 240 ball-makers in and around Tonbridge were piece workers and in 1919 won a big increase. Two years later they had doubled the earnings of 1914, but worker ascendancy was short-lived against pressure from imported cheap balls.

English firms responded typically by seeking to cut pay. It ended in a compromise, but the trouble persisted and Australian machine-stitched balls forced the hand-stitched English product out of the lucrative West Indian and Ceylon trade.

Many ball makers worked at Kent CC grounds in the summer slack season. Fred Sayers, who lived in St Mary's Road, Tonbridge, a great nephew of the famous boxer Tom Sayers, was a gateman at Canterbury for 53 years. In a rare honour for a non-player, the club held a benefit match for him in his 50th year.

Arthur Henry James Dyer, born in 1868 and always known as Peter, a son and grandson of journeyman shoemakers, was one of many master craftsmen who could make a cricket ball from raw leather to the finished article using all five skills, quilt-making, turning, cover-making, seaming and stitching.

He was the first man in England to make an 18-panel football, but the idea was pirated before he could benefit from it. When he was well into his seventies his wife would sit beside him at the dining room table by the light of a paraffin lamp mopping the sweat from his brow as he stitched a leather football inside out and struggled to force it right way round through the lace hole.

An informative book on cricket ball and bat making is *Quilt Winders and Pod Shavers* by Hugh Barty-King.

Why Jack blew out the lantern

BLIND Jack, a respected character in old-time Tonbridge, found no difficulty in delivering messages and parcels and guiding strangers to obscure locations. People said he was helped by the echo when he clapped his hands or banged his thigh as he went about.

Jack, who did not own to a surname, denied this theory and said he made a noise as a warning to people to clear the way.

One foggy November evening Jack was hanging about the railway station in hope of picking up a job when a traveller from London asked to be guided to the Powder Mills at Leigh, a difficult journey even for a sighted person — and the floods were out along the river.

Jack took the job for the proffered shilling and set off, the traveller carrying a candle lantern "for safety". Jack, having steered him unerringly along footpath and river bank to his destination, was presented with his shilling, and the lantern which was of no further use to the owner.

The traveller, astonished to see Jack blow out the candle and prepare to leave, learned for the first time that his guide was blind. Muttering that he was damned if he knew what was going on, he handed Jack another shilling and stepped thankfully through his host's lighted doorway.

History in a cloud of dust

WHEN Fred Dibnah lit his fire and brought down the Quarry Hill brickworks chimney with such immaculate precision in the summer of 1993 he erased a landmark that had been a centre of working life for generations of Tonbridge craftsmen.

Father, son and grandson often worked together, passing skills down the generations, bequeathing personal tools and moulds used for hand-crafted bricks and tiles.

As in every industrial work place, some Quarry Hill brickworkers were renowned for high jinks which often went hand in hand with skill and courage.

Darkie Bowles was such a one. This renowned prankster climbed the 112ft brickworks chimney as a young man early in the century and was spotted by the amazed managing director, Mr Catchpole, sitting on the top with his feet dangling and playing a mouth organ.

Mr Catchpole told his foreman Edward Thompson to order the man down, and summoned the trembling Darkie to his office. Instead of the sack, which he expected, Darkie was praised for his courage and rewarded with half a sovereign. His offer to go up again for a similar reward was declined.

The chimney was not popular with neighbouring housewives. Af-

Men of Quarry Hill Brickworks in 1902 showing the high chimney, a local landmark until it was demolished ninety years later.

ter years of its smuts ruining lines of clean washing, six feet was lopped off the smoking top to placate the women, many of whose husbands worked for the brick company. But the improvement was only marginal.

However, the works steam whistle which called men on and off was appreciated by all south Tonbridge as a time check in pre-radio times.

A good wage was hard-won in brickmaking, particularly when everyone was stood off in frosty weather. No chance then of walking across a field to the Old House at Home pub on Lambs Bank kept by "Squire" Ashby.

Only a few bricks remain of the pub and adjoining cottages which offered an unrivalled view across Tonbridge and the Medway.

One who stayed at Quarry Hill through bad times and good was Riley Groombridge, who learned tile-making from his grandfather in the Lavender Hill brickfield. He retired in 1952, seven years after receiving the Institute of Clayworkers medal for half a century of service.

Another long-server was Jim Miller whose father was a kiln burner at Quarry Hill for more than 40 years.

Three Thompson brothers, Percy, Bert and Stan, all specialists with particular skills, worked there and knew the seams of Wadhurst clay and Ashdown sand which made Quarry Hill bricks so much sought after. Production at peak times was four million bricks a year.

In the second world war when the works were commandeered by the Admiralty for storage, Tonbridge Home Guard did sentry duty in the eerie tunnels.

Brickmaking is over now at Quarry Hill and houses have been built where steam shovels gouged out the clay and sent it on a little railway to the 24 kilns. A note left inside the chimney by the men who built it has been preserved in the house-builders' offices.

Farewell to a landmark. The Quarry Hill brickworks chimney, toppled in 1993.

Mr Uridge had a windmill

WINDMILLS in West Kent are usually associated with the breezy Weald and the best wheelwrights operated there. But towns also needed to grind corn and Tonbridge had a windmill, although the big Medway watermills got most of the trade.

Uridge Road off Shipbourne Road, Tonbridge, takes its name from an early owner of a mill there. It was turned into wind by a horse attached to a beam at the base. Later owners of Uridge Mill were Cox, Holloway, Ridgway, and Knell who worked it last. It was pulled down to make way for houses in 1872.

The miller lived in Shipbourne Road and had a baker's shop close by.

Uridge Mill is associated in Tonbridge history with Bobby Woodman, whose business acumen belied his small size — he was only four feet tall. He worked at Uridge Mill and when his employer died set up on his own selling greengrocery and pimps (small bundles of kindling wood). He was a popular and respected figure as he bustled about the town, his wares piled on a handcart built low to suit his size.

Some years ago one of Bobby's business cards came to light. It announced: "Robert Woodman, Greengrocer and Pimp Maker, Shipbourne Road, Tonbridge". He died in his forties and is buried in Hildenborough churchyard.

Watts Cross Mill at Hildenborough was, according to William Coles Finch's book *Watermills and Windmills*, one of the few wind-powered mills in Kent working the grinding stones from beneath — like a water mill.

Every cog and wheel in this four-storey smock mill was made of wood. An internal rope turned the cap into wind. Bridger of Speldhurst built Watts Cross Mill for John London in 1812 and Richard Burfoot was the miller in 1878. Its four pairs of stones were last used in 1910.

A working mill in Stocks Green Road was built in 1928 by Commander Arthur Tomlinson as a further attraction to his Old Barn Tea-house using parts from three old mills

Better roads and access to steam power put the wind millers out of business. Some struggled on against the annual hazard of gales carrying away their sweeps, rejecting the advice of old millwrights that while a mill could continue with only two arms "it will pull her to pieces."

William Warren, last of a famous Hawkhurst firm of millwrights, estimated the working life of a post mill at about 200 years, and only half that for smock mills, which cost £1000 to build and earned about £50 a year.

Few windmills were built in Kent after 1850.

The Slype, now Yardley Park Road, with Uridge Mill seen in the right background.

A view showing how narrow the High Street was a hundred years ago. Waghorn's forge is seen, left, below the cigar and tobacco advertisement.

Celebrations in 1900 when Tonbridge Castle and grounds were bought for the town.

Tonbridge gets its own newspaper

WILLIAM Blair was only 23 when he gave Tonbridge its first newspaper in May, 1869. He was an enterprising man, though not initially popular, for his marriage to a local girl could not cancel out the disadvantage of being a "foreigner". He came from Canterbury.

He called his paper the *Tonbridge Free Press*. This intrigued local people, for his paper was not free in the sense that it was given away. He meant, in the words of his first editorial, that "No political party shall adopt it as its own; no sect shall be able to name it as the exponent of its special views."

What Blair lacked in capital he made up in confidence. He set up an office in the vacant half of a wool shop in the High Street, and expanded into better premises on the corner of Medway Wharf Road, where the Castle Hotel is now.

He kept his hand-operated printing press in a loft in the yard of the White Hart inn in the upper High Street. The publishing business which occupies the former pub named it Blair House in his memory.

The *Free Press* held its selling price at three halfpence for more than half a century, offering at first four pages, two of national news preprinted by Cassells of London, with local news and advertisements on the reverse. Like most small local journals of its time the *Free Press* combined local news from anyone who would supply it with items copied from larger papers.

Blair, fulfilling all the key roles as reporter, editor, printer and manager, soon had his paper with its bold curved title piece accepted as a local institution. Within eighteen months it was selling 500 copies.

When he had to leave Medway Wharf in 1887 to make space for widening the Great Bridge, Blair took over Ware's former post office at 129 High Street, just above the Rose and Crown, and built a printing works at the back.

Blair was never strong and was only 55 when he died in 1900. His partner, John Twort, a printer, was joined in a private company by leading local figures and major advertisers, such as auctioneer Frederick Neve and Frank East, the town's leading shopkeeper. Another director, solicitor Arthur H. Neve, contributed articles on Tonbridge history and combined them in his book *The Tonbridge of Yesterday*.

When James Donaldson, managing director of the Tonbridge Gas Company, joined the *Free Press* board, he introduced a gas engine. This remained the FP's main source of power until well after the second world war. In deference to Mr Donaldson, the *Free Press* offices and works were gas lit long after most other businesses had changed to electricity.

The paper's period of greatest popularity began with the appointment in 1916 of James Arthur Doody as editor and manager. "Pop" Doody, as he was affectionately known to scores of young journalists he trained, died aged 76 in 1947. He was succeeded as managing director by his head of printing Eric Maskell.

Since 1938 the *Free Press* had drawn strength from its association with the *Kent Messenger*, and in 1965 printing was transferred to Maidstone. This was not popular, for readers took pride in having the "Only paper printed and published in Tonbridge".

It succumbed eventually to competition from its main rival, the *Kent and Sussex Courier*, but retains a secure place in the affections of older Tonbridge people.

William Blair's first Tonbridge Free Press *office on the corner of Medway Wharf Road was lost, with the Castle Inn behind, to road widening when the Great Bridge was replaced in 1888.*

Sunday blast at powder mills

THE gunpowder mill at Leigh was a major employer for more than a century. There were sometimes explosions and over the years several people were killed.

The biggest bang occurred during — though not as a result of — a thunderstorm on a Sunday night in 1916. Houses in the neighbourhood lost their ceilings and windows, pieces of metal landed in Tonbridge and the following morning trees were festooned with rags and strips of paper. Fortunately no-one was killed or injured because the works were not operating.

The mills were founded in 1812 by a partnership including John George Children, of Ferox Hall, Tonbridge, and his friend Humphry Davy, inventor of the miner's safety lamp. They obtained a licence for the construction of "several mills and other engines for making gunpowder with proper magazines and offices adjoining and also magazines for keeping an unlimited quantity of gunpowder" on Children's land near Ramhurst mill.

George Children's involvement ended with the collapse of the Tonbridge Bank in which he was a major shareholder. He had fallen out with Davy, who also quit, probably under pressure from his new wife, a tiny woman with a violent temper whose social ambitions did not include the grubby business of making gunpowder.

The mills flourished under a surviving partner, James Burton, of Mabledon, Tonbridge, and his son, William Ford Burton. They were famous for their Smokeless Diamond sporting powder and substantial suppliers to the military. Products were test fired on a gun in the grounds.

After W.F.Burton's death in 1856 the powdermills were bought by the brothers Charles and Thomas Curtiss, passed to Curtiss and Harvey and eventually to Nobel's and ICI.

The works had wooden machinery powered by four water wheels driven by the flow from a mill pool into the Medway — a very safe system as no heat or sparks were involved. The wheels drove eight pairs of grinding stones, a hydraulic press and equipment for corning, glazing, dusting and drying. The company stored up to 2000 barrels of gunpowder in a magazine on the Thames near Erith, and leased a wharf 150 yards above the Great Bridge in New Wharf Road, Tonbridge.

Supplies for the mill and finished products were carried on barges along small canals (which can still be identified) to the main river. An internal railway served stores protected by earth mounds in distant parts of the site. Many workers lived in cottages close by. Some built in 1913 had a single door on the side away from the mill to limit damage in the event of an explosion.

It was dangerous work and sometimes workers were killed or injured. Four victims of a blast in July, 1864, are buried in Leigh church-yard. There were other accidents in 1878, 1882 and 1885, though with only one death. In 1927 two Tonbridge men, Frank Scott and Dennis Batchelor, were killed. Mr Scott, a Territorial Army soldier, was buried with military honours in Tonbridge cemetery

Many women worked at the powdermills in the first world war. In peace most jobs were done by men, and there was sadness and anxiety in 1934 when gunpowder-making stopped and some operations moved to Scotland under re-organisation by ICI. A few Leigh and Tonbridge men went north to stay in work.

In the 1920s when most men cycled to work, Tonbridge Cycling Club secured the tarmac path along the river to the powder mills as a right of way for bikers.

Song along the wire

CHARLES V. Walker, the South Eastern Railway's chief electrician from 1845 to 1882, used the telegraph lines beside the Tonbridge to Redhill line for early telephone experiments.

From his home in Pembury Road he spoke to a Redhill colleague known as Charlie and heard a boy called Frank Wells sing *Highland Laddie* over the line.

A reporter wrote: "Every word could be distinguished as plainly as though the boy had been in the next room".

The Medway Navigation Company and the Baltic Sawmills were among early subscribers to the National Telephone Company after Sir Julian Goldsmid allowed wires from Tunbridge Wells to cross Somerhill Park in 1888. Ten years later there were 21 names in the Tonbridge directory.

The earliest exchange was probably in the High Street workshop of Charles Woolley, father of Kent and England cricketer Frank Woolley and may have moved with him to East Street when road widening claimed his shop. Later the exchange occupied the first floor of the General Post Office opposite Woolworths.

One of the first business telephones in Tonbridge was installed for Charles Barkaway, butcher and grazier. Of course, only wealthier customers who also had phones could place an order with the butcher by asking the operator to ring 1Y1. It saved at least one daily round by pony and trap calling for orders.

Mary's mission to the poor

ST Eanswythe's Mission in Priory Road, Tonbridge, will be for ever associated with the name of Mary Caroline Gorham.

Youngest daughter of William Gorham, of solicitors Gorham and Warner, she was born in the house next to their offices that later became Fosse Bank School and devoted her life to the care of the needy, and particularly the poor, of Tonbridge.

She died aged 78 in 1932, too ill to travel to London to receive the MBE awarded in the New Year honours. The citation described her as "for many years the organising secretary of the Duxhurst Homes for Inebriate Women and the Home for Children at Duxhurst, a devoted worker among the poor of Tonbridge".

When a "New Town" developed around St Stephen's Church after the railway arrived, Mary Gorham identified a need for spiritual welfare among women and girls in the streets of small houses run up cheaply by the railway company and other industrial concerns.

The success of her weekly Bible class for women in a room under the former St Stephen's vicarage in Quarry Hill Road soon pointed the need for a larger headquarters. The first move entailed members climbing a rough wooden ladder to a loft over Alfred Stone's bakery at 77 Vale Road.

The class was soon so popular that it had to be divided in two, the second half waiting, sometimes in pouring rain, for the first to finish before they could be allowed in.

An appeal for funds was immediately successful and in 1890 a corrugated iron mission church with seating for 250 was opened in Priory Road and named after St Eanswythe, a grand-daughter of Ethelbert, King of Kent who helped to spread Christianity in the county.

The mission sought to gather in all who had abandoned their faith or had no allegiance to a place of worship. Its programme of cheerful, practical Christianity linked with social events, fun and recreation found a ready response in hundreds of women condemned to humdrum and lonely lives in a poor and crowded part of Tonbridge.

St Eanswythe's was the first place of worship in Tonbridge to offer such comforts as toilets and a kitchen. There were picnics and tea parties, sports and outings, and from 1917 Miss Gorham's popular lantern lectures illustrated from her collection of more than 11,000 slides of Bible pictures, hymns and psalms.

Her theme of "homely intimacy" in worship set the pattern for St Eanswythe's under the missioners who succeeded her: Major Gordon Hughman (1932-38), Frank Law (1938-43), William Stanton (1943-54) and William Horton (1954-93).

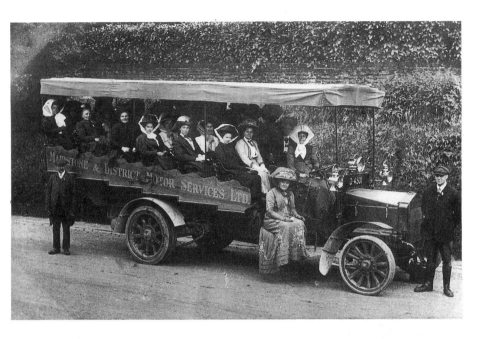

Mary Gorham, founder of St Eanswythe's Mission, seated on the running board
(above) and second from left in the picture below, on one of the Mission's outings.

High tide for a new church

FROM five men who walked out in a huff from the Independent Chapel in Bank Street, to the present fine modern group of buildings in Darenth Avenue, Tonbridge Baptist Church has served the town since 1868.

The path of progress was not always smooth. There were crises of finance, though never of faith. Then in its centenary year of 1968 the High Street church was inundated in the great September flood, precipitating a long-considered plan to move and sell the site to a supermarket.

The Baptists shared in the birth of Non-conformity in Tonbridge in 1751 when a little group of Anglican "dissenters" met in a small room behind the White Hart Inn, now Blair House, at the north end of the High Street.

Forty years later they moved to Back Lane (Bank Street) and built a new Independent Chapel in the market place. It still survives, having been in its time a Corn Exchange and a drill hall for the Volunteers and Territorials.

Richard William Annison, a grocer (whose son of the same name built a fine shop in 1899, now the Natwest Bank, on the corner of Castle Street and High Street) led the walk-out from the Independent Chapel. His strength of character was manifest in many ways; he refused to pay a rate for the upkeep of the established church and no doubt derived satisfaction from the arrival of bailiffs to distrain goods from his shop. They took several large cheeses and sold them by auction.

He was one of the four original deacons of the Baptist Church. The others were Frank East, who owned Tonbridge's leading fashion shop in the lower High Street, Henry May, who worked in the gas industry and met an untimely end in a railway accident in 1891, and Arthur Henry Neve, whose book *The Tonbridge of Yesterday* has been an invaluable source to local historians since 1933.

Disaffection with the Independents probably stemmed from quarrels over the method of baptism — sprinkling or pouring water versus total immersion. The minister, Marshall Lennox, resigned and Annison, with several others and their wives, walked out and set up a separate fellowship in a room over the old town hall on the corner of Castle Street beside Annison's shop. Annison was also treasurer of the Independent Chapel, which must have caused additional confusion.

By 1868 they had established the Tonbridge Baptist Congregational Church, though the term Congregational was soon abandoned.

They built their first church in 1872 on a site best described in terms of old Tonbridge as opposite the Bull Hotel, displacing, among others, Woodhams the butcher and his perpetual window display of a black-handled knife stuck into a large mound of beef dripping. It took the best efforts of Arthur Neve, junior, a solicitor member of the diaconate, to persuade him to leave so that building could start.

In time the church purchased the Prince of Wales beer shop next door and built a Sunday school on its skittle alley. Compensation from the urban district council for road widening paid for enlarging and improving the church early this century, and in a few years central heating replaced the original primitive coal stoves.

Among early leaders of the church were Thomas Ives, who had a cricket ball factory in Barden, and William Blair, founder in 1869 of the *Tonbridge Free Press*. He used the former meeting room behind the White Hart as his first printing works.

Others who gave devoted service included Alexander Kitchin, a Scot who was church treasurer for 35 years. He died in 1933, and is recalled as a big man physically, intellectually and spiritually, though humble and gentle-hearted.

Bernard J. Potter,a church member from 1919 until his death on the way home from church on Christmas Day, 1966, was a deacon for more than 40 years, also serving as church treasurer and Sunday School superintendent.

The notorious Tonbridge floods were endured by the Baptist Church and its neighbours almost annually, and it was, perhaps, fitting that the last great inundation in 1968 precipitated the departure from a vulnerable, increasingly inconvenient but nevertheless commercially valuable site. The newly-restored organ was under water, pianos floated and came to rest across the pews.

There were thoughts of building a church above the inevitable supermarket, but eventually the choice fell on a site offered by Tonbridge UDC in Darenth Avenue. The new church opened there on September 8, 1973, and has been considerably extended since.

Long-serving ministers in the recent past include Stanley Field (1940-1952) and David Luce, whose 15 years from 1960 included the flood and the move to Darenth Avenue.

Tonbridge Baptist Church with its superb modern facilities, extensive pastoral work and the Baptists Housing Association's warden-assisted flats seems a far cry from the disenchanted five who broke away from the Independent Chapel. But they surely would approve.

The Methodist Church in East Street, at the time of writing unused and its future uncertain, was built in 1872. The hall and schoolrooms added in 1897 were called the Victoria Hall by special permission of the old Queen in her Diamond Jubilee year.

Twopenny lesson for a pastor

IF John Row had not taken two pennies from the till in his father's shop and given them to a poor child he might never have become pastor of the Ebenezer Chapel when it was in Tonbridge High Street.

John was only four in 1809 when his mother chastised him for this "great sin against God". In a long life he was never free of "a feeling of God's presence that I could not dispel".

It came to him again at the age of nine when he and a young brother failed to own up to taking duck eggs from a nest on Lord Egremont's estate and caused the public to be banned from the park.

Apprenticed in 1819 to a grocer at Benenden, he adopted the dissolute ways of a fellow shopman, was temporarily restored through his confirmation in Cranbrook church, but succumbed again while working as a draper's assistant in Brighton.

Dogged by remorse, John Row several times contemplated suicide but returned to the fold in his next job through sharing a room with a Dissenting minister's son.

He prospered, bought his own drapery business, and married in 1829, resolving to abandon Christian thought to concentrate on success in business. Not until his wife lay dying of consumption did he return to religion.

He married again in 1849 and, helped by his wife, Elizabeth, began preaching. His business had failed and, desperately poor and with several of their six children dead or dying, he moved to Tonbridge and began taking services at the strict Baptist Ebenezer Chapel.

Elizabeth Row wrote that her husband "although by no means a gifted man, the Lord made his ministry very useful". He undermined his health by undertaking arduous journeys to distant chapels in every kind of weather.

By 1886 he was too weak to preach, and the Ebenezer's worshippers were drifting away and spirits were low.

John Row died aged 87 on November 11, 1892, and was buried on a rainy day in Tonbridge cemetery in the presence of many friends. He left notes of his life with an instruction to his wife:"Now, dear, do as you like with this after I am gone, I leave it entirely with you". As a result she published a small black-bound testimony of a man of modest talents who found peace only when he stopped resisting God's call.

John Row, Minister of the Ebenezer Chapel.

William Booth, founder general of the Salvation Army, with his son and host Frank East (right) on the Castle Terrace in 1910.

New uses for old chapels

THE old Ebenezer Chapel in Bradford Street, Tonbridge, abandoned for ecclesiastical purposes after being ruined in the 1968 flood, survived to serve many years as a furniture store and from 1993 as the headquarters of Animal Aid.

Worshippers of the Calvinist persuasion who moved to the Ebenezer (known locally as Piper's Chapel) in 1890 would be surprised — and flattered — to know that their plain little building was on offer at around £60,000 a century later.

Mr Piper, a fellmonger and substantial property owner, built the chapel after doing a deal with Tonbridge Urban District Council. Both sides felt they came out of it well.

Mr Piper belonged to a strict sect called the Huntingdons who used to meet in the Long Room behind Manchester House (later Frank East's shop on the eastern side of the High Street). His first chapel in the High Street beside Little Bridge got caught up in the council's plan for road widening. But a scheme to demolish the entrance porch was frustrated by the chapel's deed of covenant.

On legal advice the chapel asked the council to make a compulsory purchase order and offer a new site. This was done and the council, somewhat sore at having to purchase a "white elephant" for £1000, offered land just round the corner in Bradford Street, and put the old building — less its porch — up for auction.

A group of local businessmen bought it for £910 — so the council lost only £90 — and re-named it the Central Hall. Early silent films were shown there. It became a furniture store, was replaced in the 1930s by a branch of Burton's the outfitters and returned to furniture with Courts.

The Bradford Street chapel, completed in 1897, was always too close for comfort to the polluted stream below Buley's Weir. Chapel members endured the appalling smells, but they were too much in 1906 for girls of the County School (then at the Technical Institute) and its use as an overflow classroom was quickly terminated.

Mr Piper and his Calvinists never prospered after 1867 when the Baptist section split away and moved to the Zion Chapel in Pembury Road, built from the profits of a bumper harvest by Anne and Sophia Nye, of Winchester Farm, Hadlow Stair.

Another Tonbridge chapel, a grim old place in Priory Street, had many secular occupants after its Methodist owners moved out. Now handsomely converted as Kent House, it has been a cricket ball factory, a warehouse and a brewery depot.

The Methodists erected their first Priory Street chapel on the opposite side of the road, mainly for the convenience of railwaymen and their families living in the little streets close to the station.

Scouts off to camp in 1933. One of the earliest Scoutmasters was Laurence Bradley, the Urban District Council surveyor, who also founded the town's first professional fire brigade. Before there were proper scout huts he let the boys practise their skills in his garden and shed at his home, Rystone, The Drive.

Sir Charles would never yield

ARISTOCRATIC vicars were more common in the last century than this. They also tended to be autocratic and because of their wealth could leave a parish to be run by ill-paid and overworked curates without troubling to attend too often themselves.

Tonbridge parish church had such an incumbent for 52 years, Sir Charles Hardinge. Obdurate and unruffled, Sir Charles concerned himself little with the day to day affairs of his flock, considering them adequately served by the lesser clergy he employed from a comfortable distance.

Sir Charles was an opponent of change, his fixed ideas brooking no argument so that his churchwardens often counselled wearily, "Sir Charles will never yield"— and handed on a phrase to Tonbridge lore.

It apparently originated at a meeting in the Bank Street schoolroom when parishioners seeking some improvement were warned by the presiding curate, "Sir Charles will never yield". Nor did he, and a strongly supported resolution for the desired change was set aside. The phrase was in common use until the end of the nineteenth century.

When churchwardens Dove and Hodge wanted to appoint a new organist Sir Charles refused to accept their choice. The wardens stood their ground, refusing to allow anyone but their candidate to play. For several Sundays hymns were sung unaccompanied until Sir Charles did yield and accepted the appointment of Mr Dove's daughter.

After Sir Charles Hardinge, respected rather than beloved, died in 1864 thought had to be given to a memorial. A new east window was agreed as a good idea and by happy chance a suitable one exhibited at the 1862 London Exhibition was available.

However, there was a difficulty, one on which the spirit of the departed vicar ought to be consulted. The centre light represented the Crucifixion, a subject to which Sir Charles in his lifetime strongly objected.

There followed one of those bitter rows so familiar in church affairs. Group A thought the Ascension should be substituted. No, argued Group B, the Resurrection would be better.

Everyone got confused as the argument rumbled on, hardly helped by one churchwarden who demanded to know what they were talking about. When it was explained, he retorted, "Well, they're all the same, ain't they?"

In a muddled compromise the figure of Christ was removed from the cross but the Roman soldiers remained, to the confusion of visitors to the church for years afterwards. Members of the Kent Archaeological Society dismissed the mutilated residue as "a collection of coloured glass".

Hitler ended the argument with a flying bomb in 1944. The disputed window was destroyed and replaced by plain glass until a new stained glass window was installed in 1954.

Tonbridge Salvation army band in 1925 with bandmaster Fred Sayers and Adjutant Gough with his wife and little boy. The "Sally Army" had a hard time in Tonbridge -—as elsewhere — in its early days and endured rough handling from louts known as the "Skeleton Army" before incurring the town's affection.

The Poor House

BANK Street, Tonbridge, used to be called Workhouse Lane because of its principal building, the Poor House, later the National Schools. The shell of the old building has been converted into offices behind a facade preserved more or less as generations of Tonbridgians knew it.

In the eighteenth and early nineteenth century pauper women would sit outside the Poor House working flax thread on their spinning wheels — hence the term spinster for an unmarried woman. Men paupers worked in the house or carried water for washing clothes from the horsewash in the river below the castle.

In 1796 the means test which consigned so many poor families to the poor house was abolished in favour of "outdoor relief" to supplement wages or pay cottage rents. But the system was widely abused in Tonbridge as elsewhere and by the end of the century the Bank Street paupers had overflowed into various tumbledown buildings off the High Street, notably Peach Hall close to the present Christ Church.

In 1834 the government rushed through legislation combining parish poor houses on central sites managed by Boards of Guardians composed of local people of standing. Tonbridge's able-bodied paupers were moved with others from the area to a new purpose-built workhouse at Pembury, leaving only the old and infirm and single mothers with babies in Bank Street.

The Pembury guardians, emphasising the need for discipline and order, favoured retired army NCOs as workhouse masters. After several false starts their choice for Pembury fell on a sergeant of the Grenadier Guards. He failed at the final hurdle by getting drunk, though keeping his wits sufficiently to send the guardians a note declining their offer.

However, Pembury quickly settled down into a well-run workhouse, incorporating as most workhouses did, a casual ward for tramps. Until the second world war tramps could be seen at dusk burying small caches of money in the sandy soil along Pembury Road before applying for a bed. Tramps with any substantial possessions were refused admission and had to sleep rough or find a place in one of the numerous "doss houses" in Tonbridge or Tunbridge Wells.

The Pembury Union followed general practice in housing men and women in separate wards. Proud old couples would endure any hardship to avoid being separated "up The Lump", as Pembury was known because of its situation on a high bank.

Paupers received bedding, a knife, fork, spoon and basin and found themselves the concern of numerous ladies bountiful. The year-round diet, adequate though dull, expanded at Christmas into a huge blowout financed by conscience money from the better-off.

Sick paupers and people from the district who could not afford better were treated in the workhouse infirmary, from which it was alleged (unfairly) that patients only emerged "feet first". The workhouse and infirmary became part of a county hospital between the wars and some of its buildings still serve in the Pembury Hospital complex.

Plenty of people remember the former Poor House as Bank Street School It closed in 1964, the wooden floors so worn that the knots stood out like pimples.

After the paupers moved from this former parish poor house to the Union Workhouse at Pembury in 1836 the building was adapted by the National Society for Educating the Children. Although known as the National Schools it was effectively controlled by the Parish Church.

Despite its young and mostly untrained teachers, it acquired a sound reputation for instilling basic skills. Often the hard-pressed teachers would spend a large part of the morning rounding up absentee pupils, for poor attendance meant a reduced government grant.

The market just up the road and the lock-up and fire station opposite often diverted the children's attention. The school log recorded pupils being kept away for hop-picking, watching a cricket match between players dressed as clowns, helping with washing day or caring for younger brothers or sisters.

Distinguished heads of Bank Street School in recent memory include Miss Minnie Rowe, who headed the girls' department for 25 years from 1903, and George Frank Stacey, maths specialist and sportsman. He found places for many of his boys in the administration of Tonbridge. Gaffer (from his initials) Stacey was first head of the new Slade School, a magistrate, and in retirement chairman of the Juvenile Bench.

Bank Street pupils moved to a new school in Higham Lane in 1964. In Tonbridge there are still many elderly people who recall the crowded gas-lit classes in Bank Street of old.

Reaching for the stars with 'Lip' Norton

BOYS of the Judd School who were taught by Arthur ("Lip") Norton knew that his Star Atlas was a standard work, but only the few who were privileged to visit his workshop behind his home appreciated what a clever man he was.

Almost all Judd masters of the 1930s were awarded nicknames by the boys. Not to have one was a sign of pupil disapproval. Lip Norton, who disguised many acts of personal kindness under a cloak of pretended irascibility, ranked with such colleagues as Fishy, Boozer, Seedy, Bunfluff, Ossie, Tosser and Dan, presided over by Moggy Morgan, otherwise and more respectfully, The Old Man.

Stephen James, a Fellow of the Royal Astronomical Society, compiled a biography of A. P. Norton, with the help of readers who answered an appeal in the Warwick Notebook.

Born in Cardiff in 1876, Arthur Philip Norton's lifelong interest in astronomy began with his great-grandfather's gift of an old but serviceable telescope and developed when he set up a workshop in the stables of his father's rectory of All Saints, Brando Parva, Wymondham, Norfolk.

There he constructed a four-legged gravity escapement clock which ran accurately until the 1960s when it was unfortunately destroyed with others when the cases became infested with woodworm.

He manufactured everything except the optics for his early telescopes, mounting them on clock-driven equatorials of his own design. He also made many toys to amuse nieces who were living with their grandparents in the rectory.

However, he was painfully shy, especially in the presence of women, and would disappear into his workshop when a lady called — unless she was willing to join him at tennis or cycling, at both of which he excelled.

A. P. Norton completed his Star Atlas and Reference Handbook in 1910 while teaching at Calday Grammar School, The Wirral, where he remained until joining the Judd School in 1914. He set up house at 18 St Mary's Road, Tonbridge, and was looked after by a housekeeper, Mrs Hollands.

Although rather old at 38 to serve in the first world war, he volunteered but was turned down because of heart trouble. At Judd he taught geography and mathematics, disguising his shyness by an assumed air of severity, punctuated by a caustic wit. A slight lisp earned him the nickname of Lip.

Old Juddians will remember him as a stickler for detail who used different coloured pens to correct various types of error, such as spelling or grammar. He was no "chalk and talk" teacher, says Stephen James, often inviting interested boys to look at the stars through his telescope behind the St Mary's Road house and involving them in operating the school's weather station.

On retirement in 1936, Lip Norton bought one of the first new houses in Quarry Rise, where he was cared for by Miss Alethea Morphett and had his original housekeeper, Mrs Hollands, as a neighbour. He built shelves for his meticulously-indexed library of nearly 700 books and kept on his mantlepiece a miniature brass cannon that actually fired. He converted the garage to a workshop equipped with his lathe and an extensive range of tools, many made by himself, and set up his beloved telescopes in the garden. On clear nights they were uncovered for guests to study the stars.

Although a lifelong heavy smoker of pipe and cigarettes, Arthur Norton's health remained robust until his last years. He died little short of 80 in October, 1955, and is buried in Tonbridge cemetery.

His small telescope which he had given to a friend was acquired by the British Astronomical Association in 1953. There is no trace of his ten-inch telescope. The shed from which it was run out for viewing ended up as a chicken house on a local farm.

Judd second in the great race

NO Judd boy will ever admit that his school is second in anything. But it had to give best in the frantic race to be first when the Skinners Company was required in the late nineteenth century to found a middle school "in or near the parish of Tonbridge".

This happened because Tonbridge School, founded in 1553 by Sir Andrew Judde a rich merchant in the Russian fur trade, no longer even pretended to cater for local boys as Sir Andrew intended.

Inevitably Tunbridge Wells, long jealous of Tonbridge's great school and smarting over years of submission to government by the Tonbridge vestry, rushed in with plans to get this coveted second school for itself.

It quickly emerged that there could be two such schools. Wealthy Tunbridge Wells got to the winning post first with the purpose-built Skinners School in 1887. Tonbridge scrambled in the following year with Sir Andrew Judde's Commercial School in a desperately unsuitable building called Stafford House. It had no playground except busy East Street on to which the main door opened.

The first pupils were acquired from T. E Grice's little school in Hadlow Road just round the corner. William (Tubby) Bryant, a vigorous 50-year-old, was appointed headmaster with Grice as his deputy.

Flimsy partitions divided the cavernous Stafford House, a former military academy, into cramped cell-like classrooms. The drains smelled and money was short but Bryant's energy made the school so successful that by 1895 it was ready to move into new buildings on an ideal eight-acre site in Brook Street.

In this near perfect location the Judd School (as it became) expanded and prospered. Before long the names of pupils read like a roll call of tradesmen and farmers in Tonbridge and district. Boys travelled long distances by train, bus and bike to be educated by a staff of dedicated masters, all of them graduates.

Johnnie Evans succeeded Tubby Bryant as head and raised standards so that the school began to be noticed by the universities. Then came Major Cecil Lloyd Morgan, a soldier of the Great War who lost a leg in France. He gave Judd a special pride and character. He was followed after the second world war by Frank Taylor who passed on a "happy, healthy and hard working community" to Denis Rendall. He took a good school and improved it further, handing on the task in due time for Keith Starling to manage the greatest-ever Judd expansion in the centenary year and since.

George Stacey, a celebrated headmaster of the boys' department of the National Schools in Bank Street, introduced physical education and gave displays with his club-swinging teams in the 1890s.

Queen Mother at school's 400th anniversary

A few historic buildings saved their iron railings from the scrap iron drive in the second world war, but Tonbridge School was not spared. It lived with the ugly stubs of its once-handsome railings until 1953 when a new wall and entrance commemorated the 400th anniversary of the school's foundation.

The Queen Mother performed the opening ceremony, admiring the twin boars' heads, symbol of the Skinners Company, carved by brothers Stanley and Leonard Spickett They had a stonemasons business in Lyons Crescent until 1961.

Stanley Spickett found the Yorkshire gritstone used for the heads a wonderful material but very hard on the tools, calling for constant sharpening. Carving each head took the brothers six weeks, much of it occupied by the intricate detail of cords round the necks.

Spicketts also supplied Sussex sandstone from West Hoathly for the wall and white Mansfield stone for the capping.

Tonbridge High Street was decorated to welcome the Queen Mother. Overcast skies gave way to bright autumn sunshine as she inspected the school cadets and took the salute in a march-past led by Lieut Col H. M. Gray.

The royal visitor had lunch with the boys and was shown round the school by the head boy Roger Curnock and praeposter Hugo de Waal.

As always she made a special effort to ensure that the young photographers got all the pictures they needed, remarking to that she had never seen so many different cameras pointed at her.

Queen Elizabeth the Queen Mother and head boy Roger Curnock admire one of the boar's heads carved by the Spickett brothers when she opened the new entrance to Tonbridge School in 1953 to mark the school's 400th anniversary.

School chapel destroyed by fire

ALL Tonbridge shared the grief on Saturday September 17, 1988, when Tonbridge School Chapel was destroyed by fire. The exact cause of the outbreak is not known, but it probably started with an electrical fault connected with work being done on the roof.

The first warning at 9.30am from a teacher in the main building was quickly followed by others from outside the school. When the first firemen arrived the building was burning from end to end.

Six hundred pupils, who had been at a service in the chapel an hour earlier, stood in the grounds watching helplessly as 80 firemen from all over Kent with 15 engines and escape ladders fought to prevent the blaze spreading to the rest of the school.

It was soon clear that the chapel was doomed. An hour after the first alarm flames belched out of the pepper pot bell tower and it collapsed into a pall of smoke, sending a great wave of heat over distant watchers.

Treasured artifacts lost included stained glass windows and memorials to the school's dead of three wars. One of the greatest losses was the fine English oak Burns organ.

The fire fighters faced a hopeless task from the beginning. They pumped water from the school swimming pool, laid a pipeline to the Medway and used high turntable ladders to tackle the inferno from above.

Ideas for a new chapel were soon being discussed amidst much argument which went on for years. Eventually a Consistory Court ruled that rebuilding must be broadly within the old walls to a design recalling as much as possible of what had gone before.

At the time of writing, six and a half years after the fire, the chapel is nearing completion.

For the school's first three centuries, from 1553, the boys worshipped in Tonbridge Parish Church. A special gallery, built for them in the 17th century, served some 200 years until numbers compelled the building of a chapel in the school grounds. The first one, regarded as "temporary", still exists as the Old Library. The fire-damaged chapel was started in 1900 and consecrated two years later but not fully completed until 1909.

It survived a near miss by a bomb in 1940 and was damaged, though not seriously, by a flying bomb, in June 1944.

Tonbridge School chapel ablaze and the "pepper pot" bell tower about to fall in September 1988.

Funeral horses in dash to Knole

TONBRIDGE fire brigade tried hard to keep up with its richer rivals from the earliest days of organised fire fighting and horse-drawn manual or steam pumps.

Only the largest municipal brigades had horses waiting ready for a call. Others, like Tunbridge Wells, could call on well-equipped local stables. But Tonbridge, with fewer resources, was sometimes in desperate straits and had to commandeer horses from passing cabs and carts.

Steam pumps were kept ready with a little nest of dry wood chips under the boiler to be fired when a call came. Fuel was added on the way to the fire to get the pump at full pressure on arrival.

A big fire at Knole, Sevenoaks, ancestral home of the Sackvilles, taxed the resources of three towns in 1887. The reclusive Lord Sackville, having offended local people by banning them from his grounds, was lucky to have his mansion saved.

The fire started in the stables adjoining the house at eleven o'clock on a Tuesday morning. The fire bell on the top of the house was rung and while estate workers led the horses to safety and tackled the blaze with hand pumps, the Rev C. E. Few, Vicar of Seal, who happened to be at Knole, galloped into Sevenoaks to raise the alarm.

The local teams did their best, but with the flames threatening to engulf the house and its priceless treasures, the Tonbridge and Tunbridge Wells brigades were summoned by telegram at 2.40 pm.

Although Tonbridge got the call first, no horses were available to pull the steam pump. In desperation the captain stopped a funeral and took horses from a hearse and two mourners' coaches.

The Tunbridge Wells call was answered by its leading coachman Dan Hoadley. He put a team of four strong horses in the shafts of the steam pump, and galloped off to Sevenoaks. Covering the 13 miles, including the long drag up Riverhill, in an hour and 13 minutes, he passed the Tonbridge brigade on the way and beat them to the blaze.

The Chief Constable of Kent, Captain Hay Ruxton, was there with a strong force of constables ordered by Lord Sackville to keep sightseers out of the park. However, hundreds who responded to the fire bells defied the police and helped save Knole by working the manual pumps.

There was plenty of water from cisterns hidden under the flagstones of the courtyard and from a town reservoir recently completed on Lord Sackville's insistence. The family, at Scarborough and missing all the excitement, was kept informed by telegram.

The *Courier* said: "Lord Sackville has been wont to rigidly exclude the public of late years, but on Tuesday people literally saved his mansion by ignoring his exclusiveness and flocking at the first sound of the alarm in hundreds to the place, where they manned the hand engines and assisted in other ways." Exhausted firemen, still struggling with smouldering hay on Wednesday, welcomed a thunderstorm.

Tonbridge fire brigade's Salamander steam pump remained a popular performer at displays long after being replaced by modern equipment.

New brigade after tragedy

TONBRIDGE'S anger and grief after a father and three daughters died in their blazing home in 1900 led to the formation of the town's first efficient fire brigade. They could not be rescued because the volunteer brigade's escape ladder was locked behind high gates in the Castle grounds to keep it away from young hooligans, and no-one could find the key.

Mr Tatham was manager of Harris the drapers and lived in the flat over the High Street shop with his wife, son and three daughters. Father and the girls died as neighbours shouted for the escape ladder that never came.

The little boy, Tommy, was saved when a French man staying at the Bull Hotel close by urged him to climb on to a parapet and jump into the arms of people waiting below. Mrs Tatham, on the roof and outlined in flames, was about to leap when a ladder was brought to save her.

Tonbridge's volunteer fire brigade at that time was more enthusiastic than efficient, relying for call-out on boys running to the men's homes. Hoses connected to an elderly manual pump were too short to be of much use on a new escape ladder purchased to cope with the increasing height of commercial buildings.

After the tragedy the escape was kept — unguarded, but no boy dared touch it — under the old town hall until a new fire station was built in Castle Street.

The new brigade formed and developed by by the urban district council's surveyor Laurence Bradley was given a modern Salamander steam pump and firemen were trained under a full-time professional officer.

The "Sally" with its shining brass fittings was Tonbridge's favourite vehicle. It pumped out the swimming pool on Sunday mornings and was a star attraction during Cricket Week when firemen played hose soccer with a huge ball on the Racecourse sports ground.

After the Tatham tragedy a long poem "In Memory of the Late Terrible Fire in Tonbridge" was widely circulated. It claimed in these two verses that the escape could have been taken out from a smaller door:

Some have gone for the fire escape
That stood in the Castle Grounds.
They tried their utmost to get it out
But the way could not be found.

In that most terrible moment
They did not think the small door to try.
They had to leave the escape standing there
While they went back with a sigh.

The Whitefriars Press disaster

IN a century which included two world wars a few events stand out in the memory of local people to be handed down the generations. One was the fire which destroyed the Whitefriars Press on the riverside at Tonbridge in 1926. Although few can remember this great blaze directly, it is part of the lore in long-established families.

Word of the disaster spread rapidly and in the early hours of a June morning hundreds of people, many in their night clothes, stood in Lyons Crescent watching the awesome sight across the Medway.

As a fire it was probably not exceptional, but it happened in a fraught period as working people recovered from the stresses of the General Strike. Whitefriars Press with 400 staff was Tonbridge's largest employer.

At a time when all working people clocked on in the morning, went home to lunch and departed en masse at the end of the day, the High Street was full of bustling folk walking, cycling or running for buses, mingling with another tide from the second largest employer, Brown, Knight and Truscott's Dowgate printing works in Douglas Road.

On that June morning in 1926 Press workers meeting the postman on his early rounds were asked, "Where are you off to?"

"To work, of course," they replied. "Oh no you're not," said the postman, "The place burned down last night."

He was not exaggerating. Staff finding Medway Wharf Road blocked by fire engines had to stand on the other side of the river to view the ruin of their workplace. Apart from the counting house and a paper store, everything had been destroyed.

The cause of the fire, which defeated Tonbridge and Tunbridge Wells firemen after an all-night battle, was probably a smouldering cigarette end in the bicycle shed, though this was never definitely established.

The alarm was raised at 1am by the night watchman at the same time as bells connected to the firm's fire detection system went off in Tonbridge fire station.

Chief Officer Bradley, who could call on only one fire engine and ladders, put men on the roof to attack the blaze from above. Thick glass windows frustrated them until well-aimed stones from watchers broke the panes. Fire fighters in smoke helmets got into the building, but it was a hopeless battle as typesetting machines crashed through the floors on to printing presses below. Work in hand was reduced to a mass of molten metal.

The manager, Mr W. S. Minton, called from his home in Lyons Crescent within view of the works, arrived with his wife and son Albert, who was also in the business. As Mr Minton began to make plans for emergency production, anxiety switched to the adjoining Baltic Saw-mills yard packed with timber, and the gasworks a few yards away. A family in a cottage beside a gasholder was evacuated.

In his history of the Whitefriars Press, Albert Minton, who succeeded his father as manager and retired in 1962, wrote: "The three-storey building adjoining the central building on the east (gasworks) side where the fire started was soon seriously involved and the flames spread in spite of the enormous volume of water played from all angles.

"We expected to hear a big crash when the top floor (the book room) could no longer support the hundreds of tons of type and printing formes, but no such crash came. It was found later that the fierce heat had melted all the metal, which cascaded down to the ground floor, moulding itself in solid masses between the joists."

The *Tonbridge Free Press*, described the fire as "the greatest calamity that has occurred in the town within living memory".

Most of the employees apart from a few on salvage work were stood off. Many were out for six weeks. They were taken on again a few at a time when printing resumed in hired premises. A temporary composing room was set up in a former roller skating rink in Bradford Street.

Mintons managed the Whitefriars Press for nearly 50 years after W. S. was sent from the firm's London headquarters in 1907 to sort out labour problems. He soon identified "a lack of human relations", installed friendlier management and set up the Whitefriars Press Club, which still thrives.

The Medway Wharf Road works was opened in 1886 as the country branch of Bradbury Agnew to print the humorous magazine *Punch*. In 1916 it was named Whitefriars Press after the precinct of Whitefriars in London where Bradbury's first printed *Punch* in 1841.

Tonbridge firemen on parade in the early 1900s before they got their Salamander steam pump.

Another well-known printers, Brown Knight & Truscott, now departed from Tonbridge. This was the composing room and bindery at Dowgate Works in the 1920s.

Grim tale of secret tunnel

Only a few people are fortunate enough to have a copy of the beauti fully-bound *Tonbridge Legends*, a fanciful story about tunnels under the Castle written in 1856 by an unknown author. It was privately printed by Richard Ware, whose works and post office at 129 High Street became the headquarters of the town's first newspaper.

No-one has succeeded in identifying the author of the *Legends*, although he must have been known to Mr Ware's employees, some of whom acquired copies of the book. He was a person of some substance, for the printing and binding are of high quality.

The writer introduced his book as "the expression of ideas gathered from a casual meeting in the neighbourhood of Tonbridge with a man dressed in mean garb but through whose faded garments and forlorn appearance still shone the bearing of a gentleman."

In declaring in a foreword,"That the subterranean passages of Tonbridge Castle did exist I have no doubt" he was not alone. It was popularly believed until quite recent times that passages linked the Castle with the Chequers Inn and the Parish Church, though I have never understood why our forebears should have toiled through smelly, dripping tunnels when they could pop down Castle Street.

The stories, dedicated to George Stenning of Tonbridge "in token admiration for his high character", record the imagined conversations of five men stranded on a bleak island in sight of two rotting ships containing the bodies of comrades killed by yellow fever.

To relieve the tedium of their ordeal each man tells a tale. On the third night one of the group entertains his comrades by reciting his experiences as a student of 17 "learning the ways of a gentleman" from Isaac Plant Fleming at the Tonbridge Castle military school. These young men, known as Flemingites, were a lively lot, both admired and feared for their arrogance, sometimes marching arm in arm down the High Street, pushing other pedestrians aside.

The castaway's tale describes how he and his friends dug their way into a hidden entrance in the walls of Tonbridge Castle and descended 43 steps into a vaulted chamber.

A ball of twine tied to the leader's waist unravelled as they explored secret passages under the river towards the Priory of St Mary Magdalene (Vale Road), eventually reaching a smaller room where they encountered a "grinning skeleton" guarding a mouldering oak chest from which gold coins and jewels were spilling. The boys fled in terror and the narrator declared:"From that day I have never returned to Tonbridge".

The writer of the Legends certainly knew Tonbridge well, and I have wondered if his dedication to "George Stenning" disguised a tribute to Joseph Snelling, an admired "Mister Tonbridge" of his time (1820-

88). He was a bookseller, stationer and schoolmaster and, at the time of his death, Clerk to the Local Board.

Fleming's pre-Sandhurst school for training young officers had various homes, including Eton House, now Smythe House, Tonbridge School, and a bleak building attached to Stafford House, East Street, where the cadets lived in tiny cell-like rooms on the first floor overlooking an exercise area.

The last vestiges of this occupation disappeared in 1889 when the former military academy became the first home of Sir Andrew Judde's Commercial School. It was later a furniture warehouse and is now offices for Willetts the construction company and named Judd House.

Tonbridge in the groove

THE Tonbridge firm of Crystalate was a leader in the record industry in the great days of "name" dance bands, including Jack Payne. The earliest label produced by the Crystalate Gramophone Record Manufacturing Company in Cannon Lane was Imperial and the first pressing was probably two sides of The London Orchestra acoustically recorded by a large horn in the studio. Crystalate went over to electric recording in 1926. One of its biggest scoops was winning Jack Payne from Columbia in 1932.

At one shilling and threepence (about 7p) Imperial's records were half the price of rival labels and caused a sensation. Other great names recording on Imperial in the 1930s included Jay Wilbur, real name Wilbur Blanco, who had a prodigious output under many pseudonyms.

Crystalate cut more than two thousand sides for the popular eight-inch Eclipse label. From 1932, when it absorbed Aeolian, Crystalate hit the market with a new sensational "long player". Using narrower grooves, its eight-inch and ten-inch records played longer than rivals' larger discs.

In 1933 Crystalate took a new name, Rex (the King of Records) and launched Primo Scala and his Accordion Band, a creation of musical director Harry Bidgood - which wasn't his real name anyway. Most of the big band leaders recorded for different labels under other names, and sometimes, like Primo, hit the big time and were stuck with it.

Crystalate's managers were fully equal to this crazy game and kept their place at the top of the market. Their nine inch Crown discs, held down to a price to meet Woolworth's slogan "Nothing over sixpence", featured many new names - Billy Merrin and His Commanders from the Nottingham Palais de Danse and Mrs Jack Hylton's band. She was really Ennis Parkes but used the pulling power of her husband's name.

Crystalate, who sold out to Decca in 1937, is recalled with affection by hundreds of Tonbridge people who worked there. When times were hard people were grateful to be called in to meet a rush of Christmas orders.

Triple murder in an orchard

IN the summer of 1940, when Britain was steeling herself for invasion and the first shots were being fired in the Battle of Britain, an elegant woman dressed in trousers, a light blouse and a blue pullover arrived at Tonbridge station carrying a heavy brown paper parcel.

She was Florence Iris Ouida Ransom. In the parcel was a shotgun with which in a few hours she would commit a brutal triple murder.

Mrs Ransom, aged 35, known as Julie, had travelled from Piddington, near Oxford, where she lived with Walter Edward Fisher. His wife, who had also taken a lover, condoned this liaison and the couple remained on friendly terms.

This irked Julie. She wanted to be the real Mrs Fisher. She borrowed a shotgun from her brother saying she wanted to kill rabbits, and made her way to the Fisher family's cottage called Crittenden at Matfield. There in the orchard on July 9, 1940, Julie Ransom shot first 46-year-old Mrs Freda Fisher, then her 20-year-old daughter Freda, and finally their maid, Mrs Charlotte Saunders, 48, as she ran to see what was happening and was the only witness.

At first the police were totally baffled. Alerted to the tragedy by Mrs Fisher's mother, who expected her daughter to tea, they thought a madman must be on the loose and kept children in the local school until they could be escorted home.

But the clues soon pointed inexorably to Julie Ransom. She could not ride a bicycle and had tried to get her husband to teach her. She fled the murder scene on Freda's bicycle but crashed within a few yards.

William Smith, a 14-year-old charcoal burner, saw Julie Ransom clutching a brown paper parcel and "almost running" on Colts Hill, Capel.

She hitched a lift on a baker's van to Tonbridge, and was seen at the station agitated and confused by ticket collector James Botten and taxi driver Alfred Burr. They noticed she was carrying a heavy parcel.

Back at Piddington she tried to cover her tracks. But in the murder garden she had left a vital clue: a white hogskin glove. Invited by Detective Chief Inspector Beveridge of Scotland Yard to try it on, she protested that it was obviously too small. But the detective insisted and found the glove a perfect fit.

At the Old Bailey trial a jury took only 47 minutes to find Mrs Ransom guilty of murder. The judge put on his black cap and sentenced her to death.

The sentence was commuted to life imprisonment and Julie Ransom, who killed her lover's wife in the belief that he would then marry her, was sent to Broadmoor.

Cells replaced the old lock-ups

RICHARD Dance, Tonbridge's first chief of police after the era of parish constables, was also the first to occupy the superintendent's house when the Pembury Road police station and courthouse were built in 1864.

Cells under the court replaced the town's two primitive "cages" or lock-ups. These were in Castle Street opposite the Poor House (later the National Schools) and facing the tumbledown Black Doll common lodging house (the Constitutional Club occupies the site) in Barden Road.

The town at that time was officially over-staffed by point three of a constable, having five against a county calculation for its size and population of 4.7. So it was easy for Kent chief constable Captain Hay Ruxton to counter demands for more with an offer of an extra man or two "for your very own" if Tonbridge would pay £70 a year for each. At this the Local Board's enthusiasm cooled rapidly.

Supt Dance, who modelled his military appearance on the Duke of Wellington, was the father of Richard Dance who owned a saddlery next to the Chequers inn. His grandson Arthur Dance was a member of Tonbridge Urban District Council formed in 1894 and eliminated with local government re-organisation in 1974.

The elegant Tonbridge police station and court building, with homes for senior officers, opened in 1864

Defying the red flag law

ALFRED Cornell, a watchmaker and jeweller, was one of Tonbridge's earliest motorists and a pioneer in the campaign to end the tyranny of the man with a red flag who had to precede every motor-powered vehicle to warn horse drivers

Another was Harry Beckett, an irascible pharmacist, dentist and inventor with premises in Quarry Hill Road.

But neither was earlier on the motoring scene than William Arnold, who made some of Britain's first cars in his works beside the Medway at East Peckham. Like Alfred Cornell he courted prosecution to get the law changed. By stages they succeeded.

Mr Arnold first tangled with the law in 1896 when he was prosecuted for being the owner of a locomotive not operated according to the regulations in that he did not have "at least three persons to conduct the car, and one of them preceding the same by at least 20 yards...proceeding at a speed greater than two miles an hour and not having the name and residence of the owner affixed thereto".

Police Constable Heard peering through the window of his cottage on Maidstone Road, Paddock Wood, saw Arnold's horseless carriage passing with two persons on it. A clear breach of the Locomotive Act..

He told Tonbridge magistrates that the carriage was doing about eight miles an hour and when it ascended the hill over the railway "a large quantity of steam and smoke issued from beneath it".

The policeman gave chase and after considerable effort caught up with the vehicle and ordered Mr Arnold to stop.

Mr Arnold admitted that his name was not on the vehicle but produced an Inland Revenue licence entitling him to drive.

He was found guilty on four charges and fined a total of eight shillings, plus costs of about £10.

The car, the first seen in Kent, was a Benz brought over from Germany. Mr Arnold used it as a pattern for cars he made at East Peckham. They cost about £180 and were supplied to order, delivery in two months.

George Mercy, Arnolds general manager in the 1930s, recalled that even after the Emancipation Act removed most restrictions on motorists, counties were allowed to make local rules. Kent kept a speed limit of four miles an hour after some northern counties allowed 14mph.

Captain W. A. Gladwin, who worked for Arnolds at East Peckham, spent many years with Benz in Germany and was interned when the first world war broke out. On release he fought with the British army and was captured and held as a prisoner of war.

Charles Rose with the horseless carriage he drove for Dr Ievers on his Tonbridge rounds in 1902.

'Bus war' races for a penny fare

THE so-called bus wars of the 1920s when drivers for the rival Autocar and Redcar companies raced each other for penny and twopenny fares benefited Tonbridge passengers more than most.

For Redcar was Tonbridge-based and crews from the garage in Avebury Avenue were willing and doughty warriors in the battle with the larger, richer Tunbridge Wells Autocar. Inevitably the bitter contest ended in the defeat of both and their absorption by a bigger and better-organised rival.

It kept fares low for several years but led to dangerous behaviour on the main route between Tonbridge and Tunbridge Wells as drivers, urged on by their managers, raced to scoop up passengers waiting at a stop, and even barged each other off the road.

Autocar was first on the scene, replacing Hoadley's horse buses in 1909. It had a monopoly until 1923 when Redcar challenged on every route with modern vehicles in bright red livery.

Ill-feeling boiled over in 1927 in a Redcar-inspired prosecution of Autocar for operating a bus three tenths of an inch wider than the regulation 7ft 6in. After a "spiteful, mean and petty" case the magistrates found Autocar technically guilty, but showed their contempt for Redcar by imposing a derisory fine of five shillings (25p).

In other cases Redcar drivers claimed that Autocar rivals tried to drive them off the road, throwing passengers to the floor, and hogging the centre of the road to stop a Redcar getting past. The magistrates did not conceal their irritation and threw out both charges.

It is difficult now to imagine the bitterness generated in rivalry over fares costing twopence and at most fourpence for journeys of five miles and more. Yet the public took sides, both Redcar and Autocar having supporters who would wait for their preferred bus rather than patronise the opposition.

Autocar-supporting parents forbade their children to use the despised Redcar, and vice versa, often to the benefit of smaller operators such as Victor, and Ashby of Tonbridge whose "rattlers" served Hildenborough and Underriver.

When fares on the Tonbridge to Tunbridge Wells "race track" were cut to a totally uneconomic penny all the way, the winner picking up all passengers and leaving the rival company with nothing, it was clear that a solution had to be found.

An uneasy peace was established, clearing the way for Maidstone and District to step in. By 1935 the fun and the fury were over and both protagonists vanished into M & D.

Redcar carried the flag for Tonbridge in the "bus wars" of the 1920s. The depot was in Avebury Avenue.

Volunteers off to fight the Boer

Although the Boer War of 1899-1902 was far from being a wholly-approved endeavour of British arms, there was no lack of willingness to serve.

While not compelled to go, many part time soldiers of the home defence Volunteers (Territorials) went out, and some civilians enlisted for twelve months' active service.

Five from Tonbridge who put on khaki were Jemmy Flood, son of the town's first fire chief who lived at Waterworks Cottage, E. C. Heritage, George Payne, Coleman and Wilcox. Mr Heritage kept a diary of his adventures from February, 1900.

After a farewell dinner to the volunteers at the Rose and Crown, Mr Heritage was presented with field glasses by his employers, Punnetts the builders. Mrs Punnett knitted him a sweater..

The town band played Auld Lang Syne as the new soldiers, carrying gifts of tobacco, pocket books and fountain pens, left by train for Maidstone to be trained. While on the rifle range for shooting practice they heard that Mafeking had been relieved, an occasion for national rejoicing which contributed a new word to the English language, maffick, meaning to exult riotously.

The men, having been photographed on the county cricket ground by Bert Flemons of Tonbridge, sailed from Southampton in the troopship Tagus on March 16th, 1899, their initial cheerfulness in splendid weather soon collapsing into the miseries of sea sickness.

Another young soldier of the Queen, who have been on the same ship was my uncle, Arthur Chapman, whose father founded the W.J. Chapman building business. Arthur enlisted under age in the 2nd Volunteer Active Service Company and celebrated his 19th birthday at sea.

Euphoria gave way to gloom at the sight of a broken-down horse transport being towed by another ship, and the same day one of their comrades, Private Alma, died and was buried at sea.

But the voyage had many happy moments: sunbathing on deck, dolphins following the ship, concert parties, then the first sight of Table Mountain.

In camp on shore the troops' first sombre duty was guarding Boer prisoners digging graves in the grounds of a military hospital.

The train taking the soldiers to the front was engulfed by clouds of locusts. They did not bite, but caused the locomotive's driving wheels to slip. The final stage was a march, on rations of bully beef and biscuits, in a column of 3000 soldiers and a hundred wagons each drawn by 16 horses.

Unfortunately Mr Heritage's diary stopped at that point, but he survived the war and returned to Tonbridge to live happily into old age.

While they were away the local volunteers had their wages made up and received regular gifts of tobacco and other comforts from the Tonbridge War Fund. When the war ended £200 remaining was spent on a memorial to "Townsmen of Tonbridge and Old Boys of Tonbridge School who loyally gave their lives for Queen and Country and fighting in the war against the Boers to save South Africa for the Empire."

Most of those named died of sickness rather than enemy action.

The memorial on the lower castle walk, was unveiled in 1904 by Britain's hero of the war, General Redvers Buller, VC, DSO. The invitation was arranged by John Le Fleming who had been at university with Buller and whose son served under him in South Africa.

In the second world war the Boer memorial was dismantled and stored, to clear a line of fire for anti-tank guns covering the Big Bridge when invasion threatened. A move after the war to place it in the River Walk garden of remembrance with the memorials of 1914-18 and 1939-45 was defeated and it was restored to its old place.

General Redvers Buller, a hero of the Boer War, opens the memorial on Lower Castle Walk in 1904 to Tonbridge men who died. The memorial was dismantled and put into store during the second world war to give a clear field for anti-tank guns covering the Great Bridge.

How Sappers spoofed the Turks

ROYAL Engineer Territorials from Tonbridge were among the intrepid "last off" units which enabled the British, Australian and New Zealand armies to get away from Gallipoli almost unscathed in 1916.

This epic evacuation marking the end of the ill-starred campaign to force the Dardanelles and join Russia in an attack on Germany was described by a distinguished war correspondent G. Ward Price in *The Times* under the heading Last Days at Suvla.

In contrast to the bungled campaign the evacuation was a remarkable success, troops stealing away under the noses of the Turks with hardly a casualty. Much of the credit went to the Royal Engineers who rigged up an unmanned "firing line" and arranged realistic explosions to convince the Turks that the British trenches were still strongly held.

Ward Price wrote: "When the whole thing was over the last job that remained was to set a light to the abandoned stores. Volunteers did this by means of time fuses, which were only lit when the news was received...that all was clear.

"All the preparations which the Turks will find for their entry are not, however, of an explosive nature... a gramophone was put into a conspicuous place in a trench on Walker's Ridge with its needle on a disc ready to play The Turkish Patrol.

"Along the sandy beach where so many men at the landing in August suffered torments of thirst, I went back to Suvla Point. There there was a most fantastic variety of headgear and equipment. From the shore one had a splendid view of great fires springing up one after the other."

The Australians, who suffered heavily at Suvla, exploded a giant mine by remote control under the Turkish trenches a few hours before leaving, killing hundreds of the enemy.

In the English tradition of salvaging the best from a military disaster Ward Price wrote: "Although Suvla and Anzac have cost us so much in blood, it would be a mistake to regard this withdrawal as a confession of entire failure. Both are names that will take a proud place in the list of battle honours of our Imperial Army, for British troops from the farthest separated parts of the Empire there met and fought not Turk and German alone, but disease and thirst: the heat of summer and the deadly bitter blizzards of winter."

The winter experience was the worst. Men of the Royal West Kent Regiment and Royal Engineers died frozen waist-deep in the trenches the previous November. The survivors, many of whom fought afterwards on the Western Front, recalled it all their lives as their worst experience of the war.

A famous picture, Goodbye Old Friend painted by J. Matania in 1916 to raise money for war horses, was widely believed by Five Oak Green people to show a local man called Chiesman who served on the Western Front with heavy draught horses pulling guns. A copy of the picture, first used in the Sphere *and* Tatler *magazines, hung for many years in the workshop at Crittenden Farm, Matfield. Alf Baldock, who put it there, said it showed Mr Chiesman telling his friends to go on while he stayed with his dying horse.*

Playing on the tank and guns

AFTER the first world war the country faced a huge disposal problem: what to do with thousands of tanks brought home from France? Cutting them up for scrap would be a long and expensive task.

Then someone in Whitehall had a bright idea: give a tank as a souvenir to every town as a thank-you for War Savings during the four years of conflict. Tonbridge, like most other towns, accepted the offer and put on a great welcome for its tank on July 29, 1919.

The tank arrived by rail and was driven by an army crew up the High Street between cheering crowds to the Castle grounds. Amid clouds of smoke and dust it manoeuvred into a prepared place facing the Urban District Council offices and its engine was switched off for the last time.

The tank commander told the crowd and a welcoming committee of councillors how sorry he was to part with "an old lady friend" and recalled the feeling of being inside "with the Boche's bullets rattling on the outside".

WWI tanks were produced in two versions, male and female, although the difference was not apparent. Tonbridge's tank was female. The rival town of Tunbridge Wells, having accumulated more War Savings, was allocated the supposedly superior male version. It stood for many years on a triangle of grass outside the Vale Road post office.

The Tonbridge tank never moved again but remained an object of unfailing fascination to generations of small boys. They clambered over its tracks and hung on the steel sides inhaling a heady aroma of old machinery and rust through its empty gun ports.

The tank, and a collection of guns ranging from a huge howitzer to small field pieces, remained favourite playthings of young Tonbridge until they were broken up in 1938 and melted down to make more armaments in the war to come.

The barrels of those guns shone like new throughout their sojourn in Tonbridge, polished by the seats of small boys' trousers, their elevating wheels shiny from daily handling by pupils on their way to and from the National and Slade schools.

Although the tank remained in the place where it originally stopped, the guns were moved from an adjacent site to the Castle Field adjoining The Slade. Cars are parked there now.

The Tonbridge tank, presented to the town for its War Savings effort in 1914-18, arriving at the castle, where it remained as a memorial and popular plaything until being scrapped some 20 years later.

Succour for the men of Dunkirk

THOUSANDS of men saved from the beaches of Dunkirk in 1940 will always remember Tonbridge — along with Headcorn, Staplehurst and Paddock Wood — as places where people opened their hearts and their larders to weary soldiers on more than 600 troop trains.

The housewives of Albert Road and other little streets close to Tonbridge station brewed gallons of tea each day for up to 5,000 battle-stained men, French as well as British.

Wives and mothers called out, "Have the West Kents come through yet?" Mrs Lily Gammon missed seeing her son Harry, but a letter she threw over the fence was delivered by a porter. Harry did return, but was killed in action later in the war.

Tonbridge stationmaster Mr E. G. Collard and his wife organised relief teams on the platforms and were joined day and night by scores of organisations and hundreds of individuals in a week-long effort. Exhausted station staff refused to go off duty. Many, including Mrs Collard, did not go to bed for four days.

Volunteers collected more than £1000 from civilian passengers and went shopping in Tonbridge for fish and chips, sandwiches, sweets and cigarettes. Schoolgirls handed out postcards supplied by local printing firms for men to tell their families they were safe.

Relays of councillors, police, Civil Defence workers, Scouts and Guides, Rotarians, WVS and soldiers from local camps ensured that food, drink and the precious "I'm safe" cards were ready as each train pulled in.

The Southern Railway sent every available locomotive and carriage to the Kent coast ports where most of the 338,226 soldiers saved came ashore. There was no official announcement of the evacuation of an army, but compassion responded in a great wave.

Trains packed with weary and bloodied men stopped at Headcorn, Staplehurst, Paddock Wood or Tonbridge on their way to Aldershot. Paddock Wood fed them on sandwiches, boiled eggs and ham, and teams of fifteen Scouts worked on the station from 4pm till midnight. Betty Harris from Southborough arrived on her bike with a bag full of men's socks collected from friends and neighbours.

At Headcorn thousands of eggs were boiled in steel barrels beside the line. A civilian opened his case and gave two suits to soldiers clad in nothing but ragged blankets.

That was the Dunkirk spirit. More than half a century later the phrase has been absorbed into the language, and everyone knows what it means.

When it was all over Mrs Collard was awarded the MBE. She accepted on behalf of everyone who gave their all in those epic days.

Land Girls of Nightingale Farm rode these heavy BSA "Sloper" motorcycles delivering milk and eggs in Tonbridge during and after the second world war. The steel helmets, much disliked, were a strange pattern designed for civilians.

One man's view of the great air battle

FRANK Richardson saw the Battle of Britain in the summer of 1940 from his home in Albert Road, Tonbridge and from other vantage points as he went about his work or walked in the town and surrounding country-side.

Often he took his binoculars and applauded the RAF fighters dashing into the massed ranks of German bombers. For more than five months he set down the start and finish of every alert, described each action and tried to discover where bombs or enemy planes fell.

He converted his notes into letters to a grandson, Cyril Shoesmith. He lived away from Kent but often visited Tonbridge, where his grandfather was grateful for keen young eyes to distinguish friend from foe in the whirling battles high in the sky.

Frank Richardson spent his working life as a clerk with Maylams, the Tonbridge corn merchants. He died in 1947, just two years after the victory over Germany for which he longed.

His first diary entry was on July 3, 1940: "German bomber flying low over here circled three times and went off to the north. It returned, chased by two Spitfires. They crippled her and she started to come down but kept on and crashed in an orchard at Marden. The pilot's camera was full of photos, including Westerham and the airfield at Biggin Hill — the devil!"

Day and night, Frank Richardson kept watch. When German planes dropped Hitler's peace overture, *A Last Appeal to Reason*, Frank Richardson hurried to secure one from a bundle that fell on Postern sewage farm. Thousands were sold for a fund to buy another Spitfire.

As the battle intensified Cyril's grandfather assured him, "They haven't put the wind up us yet". But by mid-August he had daily anxieties for the safety of his wife when the sirens sounded at least three times a day and planes crashed all round.

He was sure local factories were being targeted: "They brought down two at Seal, two at Hadlow and one Pembury way. Some of the enemy planes shriek as they fall".

Often alerts followed each other all day and well into the night. Mr Richardson went into the country to get a better view. Thus on August 31: "A devil of an air battle going on overhead. Two waves came over like grey gnats. Saw seven, then seventeen and should have seen more if I had been lying on my back".

As August gave way to September a note of anxiety crept into Frank Richardson's diary. How long could the RAF keep it up? He was shocked when a disabled British bomber crashed on Dernier Road, ironically giving Tonbridge its first fatal casualties of the war.

As the Luftwaffe, defeated by the RAF in daylight, turned to night bombing of London, people were in their shelters for up to twelve hours a night. From his Albert Road garden Mr Richardson saw great fires glowing orange as the docks burned. Stray bombs fell on Tonbridge so often that it was hardly worth noting.

He thanked his grandson for finding him a new torch battery: "The one you gave me lasted nine weeks, so it was a good one".

By the middle of November the indefatigable observer was displaying signs of battle fatigue. His final report to Cyril on November 8 noted: "Six bombs at Plaxtol". Then the following day, a Saturday, "Alert 5.40pm to 9.40 and others at midnight and 1am. Four bombs dropped.

"I think I shall have to stop writing about it as you must be tired of reading it".

This was far from the case. Even as a schoolboy, Cyril Shoebridge recognised his grandfather's letters as a unique document. He made them available for publication in the Warwick Notebook on the 50th anniversary of the battle.

One side of Tonbridge High Street was hemmed in by barbed wire when a German invasion was expected in 1940.

Squatters raid PoW camp

Although homeless people failed in an attempt to seize the German prisoner of war camp at Somerhill, Tonbridge, on a Saturday morning in February, 1948, their action forced the authorities to act. As soon as the camp was empty families were found homes there.

The camp, built by Italian prisoners on the site of the present Weald of Kent School, was a work unit from which Italians and Germans went out to local farms. Germans unable to return to their devastated country were still there in the third year of peace.

They stared in astonishment as some 25 raiders carrying pieces of furniture and urging each other to "Get a hut" raced between the buildings. A British sergeant gave the alarm and the camp commandant, Lieut. Colonel Graham Ord, called out his officers. As they headed for an area known as the compound the raiders found themselves trapped amid a forest of barbed wire entanglements.

Colonel Ord told them they could leave through the gates but they would not be allowed back. Some stood their ground and tried to catch food thrown over the wire by Labour councillor Bill Mann. The guards threw it back.

Mr Mann tried to contact the owner of Somerhill, Sir Henry D'Avigdor Goldsmid, a distinguished wartime soldier who might be expected to support the would-be squatters' cause. But Sir Henry was away.

After five hours the squatters gave up but had made their point strongly enough for the camp to be taken over for housing after the last Germans left. Not all the PoWs went home. A few married local girls and still live in the area.

In strictly rationed Britain where food was scarcer in peace than in war the ample supplies enjoyed by the PoWs was a constant source of friction. British Land Girls also complained that the prisoners were mollycoddled, riding to work in buses while the girls walked or cycled.

In Somerhill Working Camp 40, as it was known, each prisoner received a weekly ration of 14 ounces of meat, 6oz margarine, 8lb bread, 9oz flour, 2oz tea, 8oz sugar, 7oz milk powder, 1oz dripping, 13oz oatmeal, 10oz sausage or liver, 4oz dried fruit, 8lb potatoes, 3lb fresh vegetables and 8oz dried vegetables. Harvest work earned extra.

Colonel Ord, a regular artilleryman who had been wounded in France in 1914-18, ran a strict regime at Somerhill. His formula of discipline and hard work won the respect of his German charges, several of whom wrote after the war in praise of his fairness.

Colonel Ord retired to Old Hadlow Road, Tonbridge, where he managed a large garden until well into his nineties and advised fit elderly people to do the same. He was treasurer of the Kent Federation of Horticultural Societies and ran the county show.

Somerhill Camp, built for German and Italian prisoners in the second world war, became temporary housing in the early years of peace.

Pioneer pilots planned an airfield

PROBABLY because it offered a good selection of flat fields, Tonbridge was well known to early aviators, and two of them had plans for an airfield in the town.

Frank Goodden, a well-known pilot, and Tonbridge-born Richard Johnson caused great excitement when they landed their biplane just outside the town on Christmas Eve, 1913. They hoped to open an airfield and flying school at Cage Green Farm meadows between Shipbourne Road and Hadlow Road.

But their early experience was not encouraging. When trying to take off on Christmas morning the plane tipped on its nose in the mud and broke the propellor. They had to wait two days for a replacement.

A fragment of the smashed prop was displayed in the Tonbridge Castle museum but disappeared when the exhibits were dispersed in the 1920s.

Goodden and Johnson were founders of the projected Tonbridge Aerodrome Company with the Johnson family's GP, Dr Harry. J. Manning Watts, of Salford Terrace, Quarry Hill, and a neighbour, E. J. H. Osley.

Goodden, though only 24, was a key figure as the only true aeronautical expert. Educated at King Charles School, Tunbridge Wells, he trained as an aero engineer, and in 1910 was co-pilot on a pioneering airship flight from London to Paris. He also made several daring descents in experimental parachutes.

The Tonbridge aerodrome prospectus dated February, 1914, announced plans to lease or buy a site for a landing field, hangars and workshops, producing an estimated annual revenue of £4,640, mainly from 30 pupils at £70 each to be taught by Goodden on a dual-control Gnome-engined biplane.

Goodden was also to be the main engineer, assisted by Johnson and Frank Rodgers who were partners in one of the first Tonbridge motor businesses at the foot of Quarry Hill. The three were to be paid £150 a year each, plus 15 per cent of the profits.

But seven months later the Great War put paid to these high hopes. Johnson, who had gone to Australia on a flying project, returned to join the Royal Flying Corps. Before leaving for France he circled Tonbridge three times in farewell.

He survived several air fights and the death in action of his observer before being killed, aged 27, in a crash on take-off.

Frank Goodden also died on war service testing a new plane at Farnborough.

Crowds surround a plane in which pioneer pilot Frank Goodden and his Tonbridge associate Richard Johnson landed at Cage Green on Christmas Eve, 1913. They planned a Tonbridge airfield and flying school but both were killed in the Great War.

Men of Kent or Kentish men?

I have never been able to give a clear answer as to the distinction between a Man of Kent and a Kentish Man. But a researcher for the Association of Men of Kent and Kentish Men dates it from AD 500 when settlers from the Frisian Islands colonised land north and west of the Medway and became Kentish Men, while the Jutes south-east of the river were Men of Kent.

Other versions place Kentish Men in the Diocese of Rochester and Men of Kent in the Canterbury Diocese. Natives of Kent receive their designation from place of birth, others from where they live. Women members of the association from anywhere in the county are Fair Maids of Kent.

The requirement of Kent birth was dropped in about 1950 and membership of the association is open to anyone living in the county.

Pilot's skill saved airliner

In the 1930s people were used to seeing the big Imperial Airways passenger planes flying low over Tonbridge. They were not pressurised and were not going far — only to the Continent — so they did not need to be very high.

The four-engined Hannibal, one of a fleet described as "the biggest and most luxurious aeroplanes in the world" came to grief at Tudeley in August, 1931. It was skilfully nursed to a life-saving landing by one of Imperial Airways most experienced pilots, Captain F. W. Dismore.

Passengers on the 9.43am Redcar bus from Tonbridge to Paddock Wood watched the 13-ton plane struggling to maintain height amid the rain clouds. To their astonishment it glided down and made a crash landing on Cyril Pemble's Tatlingbury Farm in front of the George and Dragon pub, tearing down a telegraph pole and leaving its tail behind.

This sensational event warranted three pictures in the *Tonbridge Free Press* . The paper had the good fortune to get first-hand accounts from three passengers who walked into the office at 129 High Street and told their stories.

One of them, a commercial traveller from Leicester, said: "We were at about 800ft when we heard a spluttering sound and the machine lurched very slightly. I understand that one of the propellors had stopped.

"Looking out of the cabin window, I saw a long field way ahead of us and thought we would land there. But we went over it, just missed a cottage and a dangerous dip in the ground and landed in a meadow close to the road.

"The machine got entangled with the telegraph wires and we carried them with us and broke the pole in two. We made a most marvellous landing in the circumstances and it is impossible to praise the pilot, Captain Dismore, too highly for the skill he displayed".

The Vicar of Capel, the Rev Henry Capel, saw the plane come down opposite his house among a herd of cows, losing its tail and dragging a shattered telephone pole through a hedge.

Seeing a puff of smoke, Mr Capel feared a major disaster until he saw a door in the fuselage open. He invited passengers and crew into the vicarage and jokingly "passed round the hat" for church funds, collecting £2. Among those who gave was racing driver Tim Birkin, one of the famous "Bentley boys". He helped keep fellow passengers calm during the hair-raising descent.

Watchers realised the big plane was in serious trouble because it was much lower than usual, and an engine was misfiring.

Thirteen-year-old Thomas Sands noticed "something fly from the front of the machine. It turned sharply to the right, the engine re-started and it glided downwards.

"The pilot seemed to be looking for somewhere to land. It looked as if he was making straight for a cottage, but in the nick of time he turned to one side."

The airliner, cruising speed about a hundred miles an hour, was flying through driving rain from Croydon, the main airport for London, to Le Bourget, Paris, when something, perhaps a bird, hit the port engine on the lower wing, throwing debris into the upper port engine and smashing the propellor.

These Handley Page biplane giants of Imperial Airways were inherently safe, carrying the British flag all over the world, Named after mythological and historical figures, they were in two groups, the 24-seater Hannibal, Horsa, Hanno and Hadrian, and the 38-seater Heracles, Horatius, Hengist and Helena.

Hundreds of people flocked to Tudeley to see the Hannibal dismantled. It was repaired and flew again only to be destroyed in an accident during the war.

The Imperial Airways airliner Hannibal which crash-landed at Tudeley in 1931. All on board survived.

Work for the jobless in the Great Depression

TONBRIDGE did not escape when the world plunged into depression after the Wall Street crash of October, 1929. But the town's long tradition of caring found jobs for hundreds who would otherwise have been on the dole.

In the harsh winter of 1932-33, a time of hunger marches, Love on the Dole and Orwell's Road to Wigan Pier, Tonbridge had more than a thousand out of work.

The government, apart from cutting wages where it dared, did little. Responsibility rested on self-help and local administrations. People in work and businesses struggling to survive did what they could, but it was not much.

So Tonbridge Urban District Council and the local Trades Council joined forces in the Woodland Walk scheme similar to one which built the River Walk in a smaller depression after the 1914-18 war.

They used a government loan of £2,000 to employ men on the dole to convert a gift of land on the former Cage Farm into the Woodland Walk from Starvecrow Hill to Higham Lane. Other schemes included hard paths round the Sports Ground — purchased for the town ten years earlier.

There was no shortage of do-gooding advice. One idea was to re-open the workhouses as centres for men to do tailoring, sewing and gardening while their wives kept the place clean. Those fortunate enough to obtain jobs outside would contribute towards their keep. The main exponent of this idea recommended a diet of good plain food, mainly soup, eggs and vegetables; not too much meat as this was not essential.

Someone else suggested a means test for employed women whose husbands also had a job, a tax on women doing men's jobs, and cancelling the tax on menservants "to encourage the employment of housemen".

All these mean-spirited ideas were rejected with the contempt they deserved and Tonbridge struggled on with its home-grown schemes to give jobless men the dignity of work.

Through its enterprise Tonbridge acquired a valuable new facility in the Woodland Walk. Eventually the economy seemed to recover of its own accord. The end of 1933 was better than the beginning. America revived and in Germany Hitler's threatening national socialism forced Britain to re-arm and set her factories humming.

"Heavy Going" was the title for this photograph by Bill Horton published in The
Times newspaper in March, 1931. It shows a Baltic Saw Mills team pulling a limber
loaded with logs out of the mud on land off Stocks Green Road, Hildenborough,
farmed by the Fitch-Kemp family. The man at the head of the lead horse is Arthur
Curtis and his companion wielding the stick is Jim Bowen. Both were familiar figures
as they guided their great waggons through Tonbridge High Street into the Baltic's
riverside yard in Lyons Crescent.
A painting made from the photograph was presented to G. Leslie Water, chairman of
Baltic Saw Mills, in 1951.

Russian prince who chose Tonbridge

FOR more than thirty years the tall, aloof figure of Prince Belosselsky, a Russian aristocrat who fled the revolution in 1917, was familiar to Tonbridge people. He enjoyed a drink in the Rose and Crown hotel, grew sweet peas and gave prizes for garden shows. But little else was known about him.

I cannot better author Denton Welch's description of the old prince walking in Tonbridge "with an extraordinary and studied air of elegance...the sweep and the sway, the curious lilting and at the same time padding gait, a sort of imperial waddle, the feet pointed outwards and the head held stiffly; the flowing clothes, the jacket very long, the trousers very narrow, the soapstone rather eskimo face with many wrinkles, and hawk eyes.

"There was snobbery in every movement and line, but also care, thought, discrimination, idealism and beauty".

The prince invariably wore suits of some thin khaki material, beautifully polished brown and white shoes and a drooping pointed trilby.

The picture of this fine old Russian gentleman stranded in England and eking out a precarious living by selling pieces of furniture and carpets he had carried into exile, was completed for me by Constantine Lomakin, of Hadlow, whose father was the prince's valet.

The prince had been a colonel in the Czar's army. He was still a fine horseman in old age and hunted and played polo on the former Penshurst airfield.

The Lomakin connection with Prince Belosselsky began with an incident worthy of the plot of a Russian novel. A Ukrainian peasant boy working in a forest, found a gold watch after a hunting party had passed and sought out its owner. He was Prince Belosselsky, father of the Tonbridge prince.

The old prince rewarded the boy's honesty by giving him a job in his stables. Lomakin did well, rising to coachman, then valet and travelling widely with the young prince. After the revolution and the murder of the Czar and his family Lomakin fled with the prince to Finland, then to Paris, London and Tonbridge.

Constantine Lomakin was born in Petrograd and came to England with his parents at the age of ten, sharing with them the various homes where they worked for Prince Belosselsky and his American wife Princess Susan. One of their two sons, Andre, was at Tonbridge School from 1923-28 and took Russian as one of his School Certificate subjects. Because no-one at the school spoke Russian, Andre's father was allowed to give the oral dictation.

At the Belosselskys' first Tonbridge home, Mill House, Mill Crescent, the staff included an English butler, Princess Susan's maid, Mrs Ambramova, and Mr and Mrs Lomakin.

The family fell on hard times after the Wall Street crash and moved several times — to Hilden Grange, to Homeleigh, 20 Hadlow Road next to the Mitre pub and to Dry Hill Park Road, selling their furniture piece by piece.

Constantine Lomakin remained fluent in Russian and recalled the prince as "a very military man, gruff but always friendly".

After Princess Susan died aged 60 in 1931 from an illness caused by her heavy smoking, her husband moved to a flat in Lyons Crescent where he was looked after by Mrs Ambramova. She observed the courtesies of old Russia, always bowing as she retreated backwards from the prince's presence.

Prince Belosselsky died in April, 1951, aged 83 and is buried beside his wife in Tonbridge cemetery. The Vicar of Tonbridge, Canon Russell White, gave special permission for the coffin to lie open in the Parish Church on the night before the funeral in accordance with Russian Orthodox custom.

Mr Lomakin the valet died in 1968 at the grand old age of 95. One of his grandsons gave his children Russian names, Natasha, Tanya and Nikolai.

Prince Belosselsky, a refugee from Russia after the 1917 revolution, made his home in Tonbridge.

Family hopping bought new clothes

HOPS and hop-picking are still part of family lore in many homes in Tonbridge and villages around, even though few now don their oldest clothes and wait in the dewy early morning for transport to the farm.

Not so many years ago the long summer break from school was known as the "hopping" holiday. If picking began late or lasted longer than usual mothers would delay their children's return to boost a family's earnings — a throwback to the time when farmers expected a worker's whole family to be available at key times such as harvest.

Introduction of the hop-picking machine soon after the second world war gradually eliminated hand-picking, and with it the annual invasion by thousands of London East Enders for their working holiday in the hop gardens of Kent.

They poured out of stations at Tonbridge, Paddock Wood and other villages pushing old prams and wooden carts loaded with bedding, pots and pans and treasured knick-knacks. Farmers sent trailers and waggons to meet them.

Some local families — and even a few Londoners — still find hop work in September. But the days of the bin to be filled and arguments with the tally man accused of pressing down too hard on his measuring basket are over.

For families such as the Holmes, the Shoebridges of Tonbridge, the Mitchells of Hadlow, and many more, hop-picking was an experience enjoyed by generations. Small children learned the skills from watching grandma's busy fingers, resenting but usually achieving the task of filling an opened umbrella before being allowed to go off and play.

Hop-picking transformed villages such as Paddock Wood, East Peckham and Hadlow for four to six weeks every year. Pubs prepared as if for a siege, designating hoppers' bars so that regulars would not be disturbed. Sometimes beer tankards were secured by a chain through the handles. Or pickers' beer would be served in jam jars.

Village shops erected wire netting screens across their counters to guard against pilfering. Saturday nights were always noisy and occasionally violent when hard-drinking London dockers visited their families. The Red Cow at Tudeley (it now has a new name) was a favourite place for a real London knees-up at week-ends.

In Paddock Wood the Kent Arms pub near the railway station (renamed the John Brunt VC after a local war hero) provided lunch-time refreshment for bakers who came down from London and worked a long day making bread for the pickers.

Other traders emigrated with their London customers for the season, setting up street stalls. Fishmonger Tommy Calmer traded under paraffin flares outside the Kent Arms, assisted by a legless local man,

Charlie Beach.

Hopping tradition usually featured a "strike" for a better rate of pay before picking began. The farmers, of course, set a deliberately low figure, knowing it would be challenged, and agreement was usually reached swiftly after mutually enjoyable haggling, although disputes about fair measuring would continue.

Poor families sent their children back to school warmly clad thanks to their hopping earnings. In Maidstone on the last Saturday the streets would be littered with old clothes discarded when the children climbed, clad in their newly-purchased best, on to the train back to London.

A few families always stayed on for leisurely post-hopping holidays in huts made comfortable with equipment and knick-knacks from home. By-laws stipulating that they must be vacated by November 30 were relaxed in the second world war when hopper huts provided a safe and familiar refuge from the London blitz.

Few strangers visited the hop gardens during the busy period, for time-wasters were not welcome. A man, particularly if he happened to exude an air of affluence, would be accosted by a group of sturdy women and have his shoes brushed with a hop bine. Their demand for him to pay a "footing" meant a substantial contribution from his purse, rewarded in turn by a firm kiss.

Anyone who protested would be upended into a picker's bin and given a good shaking.

One of several East End parish priests who went hopping with their flock was Father Richard Wilson, from St Augustine's, Stepney. From 1890 he travelled on the train to Paddock Wood and walked with his people to Five Oak Greeen, sleeping in a barn and washing like them in a bowl in a field.

One day after meeting a young girl who had walked five miles carrying her sick baby to a doctor the Hoppers' Parson decided that something must be done for the poor Londoners. It was not unusual for babies to be born in hopper huts with grandmothers acting as midwives.

The following year Father Wilson rented a cottage at Five Oak Green and staffed it with three nurses brought from London. They had to deal with an outbreak of smallpox as well as other ailments and emergencies.

The year after the little hospital expanded into a second cottage, and in 1910 Father Wilson moved his nurses into the disused Rose and Crown public house and called it the Little Hoppers Hospital. He altered a sign to read "Fine ales, stout and porter NOT sold here" and built a children's ward on the skittle alley.

Staff sent from the hospital in Whitechapel Road were helped by Red Cross volunteers. In time the hospital became a community centre for pickers, the courtyard with its great open fire transformed at night into an open air theatre with plays and concerts.

As public medical services improved the Little Hoppers Hospital became a holiday home for East Enders and lives on in the memory of Father Wilson and Alexander Forsyth Ashes, his successor at St Augustine's.

The round oast house for drying hops so familiar in Kent, was developed from early kilns in barns, the fumes escaping through a hole in the roof. The first wind-turned cowls appeared on square oasts, but by the middle of the 19th century round oasts predominated.

Estate employees and local builders became skilled in building the steep roofs on sturdy walls rising from foundations of great stones. Hundreds of oasts have survived for conversion into homes because they had to be well built to endure the heat of the fire in the lower part and the weight of hops piled on the "hair" held on the joists of the upper floor.

The art of constructing a cowl up to 8ft high balanced on a central pole and turning easily with the breeze has been handed down and can be studied at the Whitbread Centre at Paddock Wood. Each cowl is individual, matched to the roof it serves.

Old Thomas hid from the world

THOMAS Kibble was a very strange man. Standing hardly more than five feet, he lived alone in the late 19th century in the vast Greentrees mansion facing what is now Higham Lane, Tonbridge.

He had extensive greenhouses and farmed some 300 acres beside the road near Hadlow Stair.

Numerous stories were told about him. Some said he shunned society because he was crossed in love. Certainly his behaviour was odd.

Twice a year he would order a carriage and emerge from Greentrees dressed in spats and top hat to spend a week in London.

On returning through his great iron gates he would disappear, seen only by his long-suffering staff of several maids and gardeners. They found him so eccentric that one by one they left, leaving only a housekeeper.

He ordered tradesmen to make their deliveries before ten o'clock in the morning and had his housekeeper wait at the front door to pay them. If he heard so much as a footstep of a passer-by he would dive for cover.

Finally the housekeeper could stand no more and left the old man to do his own cooking. This was his undoing. He let a frying pan catch fire and his beautiful mansion burned down, leaving only a few walls and the remains of his greenhouses. The strange Mr Kibble moved into a cottage close by.

Nurses from the East End and some of their patients at the Little Hoppers Hospital converted from a former pub at Five Oak Green.

Pursuit of a fleeing heiress

GENTLEMAN Robert Jeffreys, so called to distinguish him from lesser persons of the same name, was confined to bed in Tonbridge with one of his frequent bouts of ill health in 1789 when his wayward heiress daughter Elizabeth, aged 16, eloped with a lover.

Elizabeth, despairing of her retired father's unexciting ways, sometimes went to the Wells in search of livelier company on the Walks. There she met George Ashworth, a Londoner who combined a keen eye for a pretty girl with a course of the spa's restorative waters.

He struck up an acquaintance with Elizabeth and, explaining that lodgings were difficult to find in Tunbridge Wells, took rooms in Tonbridge to be near her.

He made friends with her father as the next step in his plan for marriage to a rich heiress. Mr Jeffreys, immersed in his books and suffering from a chill, for which Dr Thomas Hankins was attending him, suspected nothing.   Mr Jeffreys, also nervous of smallpox which was about in the town, was confined to bed and knew nothing of George and Elizabeth's dash for London in a fast primrose coloured post chaise hired from Aaron Winton of the Rose and Crown hotel.

They were well on their way without being missed and might have got clean away had not Elizabeth's brother Henry arrived on the evening coach from London.

Calling on his father, Henry quickly suspected that Ashworth had made off with his sister. He obtained confirmation from Dr Hankins who lived next door to the Rose and Crown and had seen the couple set off in the dusk of a November afternoon.

Henry, a man of action and resource, set off in pursuit in another post chaise accompanied by Dr Hankins. They got news of the fleeing lovers at each toll gate, and caught up with them at Locks Bottom.

Arthur Neve, relating the story in *The Tonbridge of Yesterday*, says that after some little argument Elizabeth was persuaded to return to Tonbridge with her brother. The chastened Ashworth was arrested on a charge of abduction and brought before the Tonbridge magistrates.

When the chairman George Children asked if he had any profession, Ashworth replied that he had a patent for improving the steam engine. Mr Children treated him to a wry magisterial smile and commented, "You may perhaps have a patent for what you mention, but I should expect none for stealing young ladies away from their parents and guardians."

Ashworth protested, "I did not steal her" and was remanded to await further evidence. Unfortunately the outcome of the case is not known.

Elizabeth, her virtue intact, found another suitor and shortly after her escapade married the Rev Dr Stevens. They had two children and lived to a good age at Great Lodge, Pembury, which they sold to Sir Edward Colebrook, and Southfields Park, where Skinners School has its playing fields.

Dr Hankins bought Dry Hill House (later called Manor House) and died there in 1807. His widow sold the house to James West, whose family held it for more than seventy years. Ashburnham Road was built in part of the Manor House grounds and recalls the name of one of them, William Ashburnham West.

* Although Neve is firm on Tonbridge as the location of the Elizabeth Jefferys adventure, the *Maidstone Journal* placed a suspiciously similar "daring violation of the law" in Tunbridge Wells, describing the attempted abduction of a Miss Jeffery by two "gentlemen" and "a shabby looking servant" and their subsequent arrest after a neighbour raised the alarm.

In this version, old Jefferys had died and the daughter, named as Anne, stood to inherit £50,000 on the death of her mother.

However, it is too good a story to miss, and I repeat it in confidence that Arthur Neve was not given to invention or exaggeration.

A great love story of 1914

UNTIL Jonathan Smith's book *Wilfred and Eileen*, and the television series it inspired, few people connected Wilfred Willett, former secretary of Tonbridge Trades Council, with one of the most poignant stories of the Great War.

Wilfred, having given up his medical studies to fight for king and country, was hit in the head by a sniper's bullet in the early weeks of the war. His life was despaired of, until his courageous young wife Eileen crossed to France, argued her way into the hospital where he lay, brought him home and nursed him back to what could pass as health.

Jonathan Smith, a master at Tonbridge School, wrote his book after hearing the story from a pupil who was a grandson of Wilfred and Eileen.

A brilliant man, Wilfred Willett was severely disabled in movement and speech but became renowned as a scholar and writer on natural history. He lived at The Rosery, Matfield, joined the agricultural workers' union, and ignored family disapproval to sell copies of the Communist paper the *Daily Worker* on the streets. After his death in 1961 fellow trades unionists placed a seat in his memory in the Castle grounds.

Wilfred had a second claim to fame — although he never made anything of it. He was a nephew of William Willett, head of the family building firm and inventor of Daylight Saving, which became his passion. He neglected the business to pursue his idea and died the year before it was adopted in 1916 to save artificial light in war factories.

Frank Woolley, the Kentish Hop Pole

NONE of his sixty-four Test Match appearances for England was more important to Frank Woolley than the matches played with his three brothers on the earth floor of the yard beside the family home at 72 High Street, Tonbridge.

These were the games remembered by Frank Woolley when he returned in old age to the town of his birth. They followed an unchanging pattern: the two Fs, Frank and Fred, and the two Cs, Charles and Claude, taking it in turn to be England, Australia or South Africa.

They ended when Frank, his left-hand spin already hinting at glories to come, let go a flyer in frustration after Claude had defended the wicket chalked on their father's workshop door for a whole week. A broken bedroom window saw both sides banished to an alternative ground on a grassy path leading to Bartram's Brewery — now the River Walk. But it was never the same.

In summer the boys spent more and more time perched in their personal pavilion, the great Woolley Tree overlooking the Angel Ground just across the High Street. Each brother occupied a branch carved with his initials as they watched their heroes playing for Kent or being coached in Tom Pawley's Angel Nursery.

They studied the style of Colin (Charlie) Blythe, one of the greatest slow left-arm bowlers the game has known. He and Frank Woolley combined in one of Kent's most effective partnerships.

Frank Woolley was born in Tonbridge in May, 1887, the fourth son of Charles William Woolley and his wife Louise. Charles worked first in his father's cleaning and dyeing business, spending long hours perched on a ladder checking the temperature of the 12ft high copper boilers. He also cleaned the chimneys.

Frank attributed his father's reputation for sagacity and profound thinking to this early experience.

Charles Woolley set up his own engineering business at 72 High Street where the family home, a former farmhouse, and his workshops were ranged around a large earth-floored yard. A close family life behind high wooden gates to the High Street suited Mrs Louise Woolley whose unusual height of more than six feet made her shy of company.

Charles Woolley made bicycles to order, graduating from crude models with iron rims on wooden wheels to sparkling beauties on rubber-tyred wire wheels, the frames enhanced by a thin gold line applied by their creator's unerring hand.

He built his boys a little yellow and black carriage drawn by two cream goats. Charlie, as the eldest, invariably took the reins as they drove about Tonbridge. Charles Woolley's perfect little model locomotives were one of the sights of Tonbridge running on a track in the win-

Frank Woolley, "the Kentish hop pole" as a young batsman at the Angel Nursery, Tonbridge.

dow at Christmas.

The family's close friends were Mr and Mrs Herbert Huntley, who had the Bull Hotel opposite. It was the Huntleys who brought a ladder and baskets of food when the Medway flooded the Woolleys' ground floor and drove the family upstairs. Mrs Huntley always saved something from her hearty farmers' lunches to fill up Louise's hungry boys.

Frank and his brothers — who did not allow him to play cricket with them until he was six — went to the Wesleyan School in Barden Road. Frank was put down for Tonbridge School, but when the time came another opportunity was on offer. Tom Pawley invited Charles Woolley to enrol fourteen-year-old Frank in the Tonbridge Nursery on a half-day basis. This was accepted, and Frank was grateful to miss the bullying endured by tradesmen's sons who got to The Big School.

The young cricketer, an awkward figure with his six foot height and spare frame, played his first game for money when Roughway found themselves a man short against Tonbridge. Tom Pawley, the Tonbridge skipper, offered "young Woolley" and rewarded him with half a crown.

When Frank was ten the brothers spent their pocket money on a wooden red-painted cricket ball and got up a team to play Leigh Green. All went well until Claude hit the ball into a swamp. There was no spare and the game had to be abandoned.

Frank Woolley first played for Kent at the age of sixteen, watched by his proud parents and immaculate in white flannels prepared by his mother. At 6ft 3in he was soon dubbed "the Kentish Hop Pole".

Despite the handicap of club feet discovered when he played football for Tonbridge, Frank Woolley went on to become a brilliant batsman and bowler for his county and England. As a slip fielder, particularly to the bowling of Kent's Tich Freeman, he has never been surpassed.

Once he settled into an innings, runs came in a seemingly effortless flow. It was said of him: "No batsman has ever made so many runs so consistently at such speed and with such ease and grace".

The Times described his 100 in 101 minutes at the Oval in 1922 as "a sedate innings" by Woolley standards. One of his 145 centuries for Kent, against Hampshire on the Angel in 1906, won him a box of chocolates when he responded with 116 to local builder Jack Elkington's bet that he would not reach a hundred.

After losing his High Street shop to road widening at the turn of the century Charles Woolley moved reluctantly to Avebury Avenue, then to East Street. Although he lived to be more than a hundred, he never recaptured the joy of No 72.

Frank's eldest brother Charlie was an invalid after being badly wounded at Gallipoli in the first world ward. Claude saw his hero Charlie Blythe — who need not have joined up because he was over age — killed beside him in France by a shell. Claude became opening bat for Northants, playing 326 times between 1913 and 1931, making 15,553 runs. Fred, a fine engineer and too valuable to risk at the Front, spent the war making aeroplanes. Frank's value as a sportsman kept him on home service attached to the Royal Navy.

Frank Woolley played 32 years for Kent and England and was one of the giants of the game. He featured in many of Kent's glory days, including 185 partnered by Arthur Fielder, 122, in a total of 555 against Worcester at Stourbridge in 1909. His feats on the Angel ground included a mighty six reputed to have reached Paddock Wood in the back of a passing coal lorry.

He retired from county cricket at the age of 51 in 1938 with a century before lunch at the Angel. His cricket school in Stocks Green Road. Hildenborough, where he imparted his matchless artistry, was taken over by an evacuated glass factory during the war and eventually demolished.

I had the pleasure of entertaining Frank Woolley and his second wife Martha to lunch on his last visit to Tonbridge in 1976. He was saddened to find a supermarket where the Angel Hotel had been and confused by the Sports Ground. It was the Racecourse in his day.

Cricket brought Woolley fame, but never wealth. Between the wars he got £5 and later £10 or £11 for a county match, plus £1 bonus for a win. Home Test matches paid £20, and no expenses. He always resented the old rule — abolished in Kent by a captain Jack Mason — that Players (professionals) and Gentlemen (amateurs) had to enter the ground by separate gates.

Promotions, including signing bats for Duke and Sons at Penshurst, brought in valuable extras. Tips on property investment from a wealthy Kent member made Woolley's retirement more comfortable than he feared it might be. He died in Canada in 1978.

In his cricket career he scored 58,969 runs, averaging 40.75 an innings, hit 145 centuries, had a thousand runs in a season 28 times, took 2,068 wickets at an average of 19.85. He played in 64 Test matches, average 36.07, hit five centuries and took 83 wickets at an average of 33.91.

At the height of his fame surgeons asked him to bequeath his left hand for research so they could unlock the secret of his baffling spin. He never agreed, and in any case outlived them all.

There are memorials in Tonbridge Parish Church to Frank Woolley and his hero, Colin Blythe, and roads in the town are named after them.

The mystery of Devon Loch

WHEN the late Peter Cazalet trained racehorses for the Queen Mother at Fairlawne, Shipbourne, word soon got round when she had a "good thing". Such a one was Devon Loch in the 1956 Grand National, a fine horse with a top jockey, Dick Francis, later better known as a best-selling novelist.

Devon Loch's dramatic fall 50 yards from the winning post is now racing history. As he went down with the field strung out behind, Dick Francis hurled away his whip in frustration and all the local money on the greatest steeplechaser the Queen Mother ever owned was lost.

More than 30 years afterwards I talked to Johnny Hole, one of Peter Cazalet's most trusted lads who had special responsibility for Devon Loch.

He saw Dick Francis follow the race plan worked out with Peter Cazalet — hold off over the first mile, then let the big Irish-bred gelding use his intelligence, courage and enormous strength to go through the field. There were only 29 runners, and four fell at the first fence.

Devon Loch passed horse after horse. At the Canal Turn he was going so well that Francis had no need to push him.

Armorial II was in front, but fell, and Eagle Lodge took up the lead. Devon Loch passed him, and three fences from home had his nose in front, striding perfectly and going on to win.

John Hole ran to The Chair fence to watch his special horse go into the home straight. Then suddenly came a hush in the enormous wall of cheering. John ran on to see Devon Loch sprawled, his legs splayed out. He suddenly "sat down", as the radio commentator said, unseating Francis. All had been won. Now in an instant all was lost.

John ran across the course to Devon Loch, closely followed by Bill Braddon, the Fairlawne head lad. The horse was back on his feet, fit and still full of running.

To this day no-one can say for certain what happened to this "most courageous and noble horse", as Dick Francis described him in his autobiography *Sport of Queens*. The vets confirmed that physically there was nothing wrong.

The most popular theory was that he was startled by the great volume of cheering for the Queen Mother. To John Hole there was no sure answer; one of those enigmas of racing to be written about but never explained.

Francis was invited to the Royal Box, where the Queen Mother, as upset as he was, said, "That's racing, I suppose."

For Peter Cazalet, who died in 1973 at the age of 66, the disappointment must have been immense. One of the most successful National Hunt trainers of all time, he won almost every classic race, except the Grand National.

John Hole from Fairlawne stables, Shipbourne, leads out Devon Loch before the Queen, the Queen Mother and Princess Margaret for the 1956 Grand National. With only yards to go and the race apparently won, the Queen Mother's horse inexplicably stumbled and fell, unseating his jockey Dick Francis.

The night Tonbridge almost went under

NO-ONE who was there will ever forget the night of Sunday, September 15, 1968, when a wall of water four feet high swept into Tonbridge High Street. It poured into adjoining streets, marooning scores of families in their upper rooms.

After a very wet Saturday and a night of relentless pounding rain, the Medway threatened. For hours thick walls built ten years earlier along the River Walk enclosed the brown torrent. Then came an enormous surge and the flood poured over.

Within minutes Tonbridge High Street was overwhelmed. Strangely, the street lights stayed on to illuminate the contents of shops bobbing on the tide. Monday morning offered brilliant sunshine and an incredible sight. The High Street, from Lyons Crescent to Avebury Avenue, was awash and every shop was inundated. A frightening tide roared under and over the Great Bridge. All the factories and works east of the town were flooded. Cannon Bridge was washed away, carrying with it the town's main sewer.

Boats pulled to supposed safety in the riverside boathouses were swept into the main street, shattering shop windows. Ropes were rigged to get people across the torrent. Heavy vehicles brought in by the army created waves and added to the damage.

For a time Tonbridge could only be approached from Tunbridge Wells, where news of the disaster was greeted with incredulity.

The trouble was caused by nearly four inches of rain in 48 hours falling on ground already saturated by five inches which had fallen earlier. Flood warnings were issued and Tonbridge braced itself for one of its routine inundations, perhaps affecting the Sports Ground, Botany and a few other places.

But by 9pm, the High Street was flooded a foot deep and two hours later the whole street was a mill race, negotiable only by a few buses and large lorries. East Peckham, Hadlow, Paddock Wood, Edenbridge and scores of other places were equally hard hit. A new estate at Hildenborough was flooded to the tops of the ground floor windows.

The great flood of 1968 changed the face of Tonbridge. The Angel Hotel on the corner of Vale Road and adjoining shops had to be pulled down. We lost the Baptist church and the former roller skating rink in Bradford Street.

Experts are confident that such a disaster can never happen again. Since 1980 Tonbridge has been protected by the Leigh flood barrier. In several big storms since it has held the water back to be released gradually through a much-improved river down to Maidstone and on to the sea.

Struggling through the High Street on Sunday night in the 1968 flood and (below) the morning after.

Double triumph for Spender-Clay

TWO parliamentary elections in 1910 endorsed Tonbridge Conservatives' choice of Herbert Spender-Clay as the man to strike back at the Liberals. He became a popular MP and held the seat until his death in 1937.

It was a sweet revenge for the Tories four years after the Liberal Arthur Paget Hedges ousted Arthur Griffith Boscawen. Foolishly Boscawen sulked and went off in a huff to South Africa — and regretted it ever afterwards.

He blamed "bad advice, and being somewhat piqued at my defeat", although he got back to the Commons for another constituency in 1910.

This display of petulance cleared the way for the Tories' new hero Captain (later Colonel) Spender-Clay. In the January poll he converted the Liberals' 1906 majority of 1,283 into a Conservative margin of 3,210, and held the seat by 2,127 in December.

The elections saw the local newspapers locked in uncompromising strife with no pretence of impartial reporting, the Conservative *Courier* against the Liberal *Tonbridge Free Press* and *Tunbridge Wells Advertiser.*

The bitterness in print reflected Tunbridge Wells' long-standing irritation at still having to share the Tonbridge constituency. It did not get an MP of its own until parliamentary boundaries were redrawn in 1974.

When the January result came out the *Advertiser* commented sourly: "It is all over. Food taxing and Peer rule have been accepted by the electorate of the Tonbridge Division".

Riding in a motor car was a novelty for most voters. They rejected the more familiar carriages and traps to be carried to the polls in a stream of handsome vehicles, mostly Conservative-owned.

Latecomers, hoping to join a huge crowd awaiting the declaration of the January poll at Tonbridge Castle, found the gates locked against them. The police anticipated trouble from an excited mob surging about the High Street.

A great cheer drowned Liberal boos as Spender-Clay stepped from a window on to the flat roof of the council office porch, followed by a disconsolate Hedges.

The victors carried their hero in triumphal procession to Tunbridge Wells, while the Liberals, defiant in defeat, took comfort from their party's success in the country at large.

The streets of Tonbridge and Tunbridge Wells were in turmoil for hours on the second polling day in December, rival crowds roaring support for their favourites. But cries of "Good old Hedges" as the Liberal candidate and his wife toured the streets could not disguise the certainty of another Conservative victory. The Tory electoral machine was rolling inexorably, their cars streaming to the polling stations laden with delighted passengers.

Hedges might cup his hands and cry "We are winning all along the line" but he could smell defeat for the Blues (the Liberal colour then). No-one pretended that it was a gentlemanly contest, Spender-Clay being forced to deny a Liberal charge that he paid low wages — as little as two shillings a day — to his agricultural employees. It was an absolute lie, he said, and what was more his men received pensions when they were too old to work.

Tonbridge had no doubts about Spender-Clay. They sat him on a chair on top of a large motor car and cheered him through the streets, jeering at the Liberals' consolation claim on a poster outside their committee rooms: "Tory majority reduced by 1,083".

A chair tied to the top of a car was Herbert Spender-Clay's victory seat in the election of January, 1910.

Len gave the Tories a scare

THE Conservatives, confident in the security of the Tonbridge parliamentary seat, got the fright of their lives in 1956 when Labour put up Len Fagg against the Tories' Richard Hornby, imposed on the constituency by Tory Central Office in place of the popular Gerald Williams, who had given up for health reasons.

At that time, and until parliamentary boundaries were changed in 1974, the Tonbridge constituency included Tunbridge Wells — much to that town's annoyance.

The redoubtable Len, ex-sailor, Post Office worker and chairman at various times of the Labour Party branches in Tonbridge and his home village of Pembury, ran Richard Hornby close enough to leave the result in doubt until the returning officer announced the figures.

It was too close for comfort for the Tories: Hornby 20,515, Fagg 18,913 in a very low poll.

Fagg, a classic local Labour hero, had done well against Gerald Williams in the General Election the year before. Labour also had good memories of 19,525 votes won by local councillor Brian Clapham in 1950.

They stayed with home-grown talent for the next two general elections after Fagg's fright, challenging an undoubted safe Tory seat with Tonbridge School master Ken May in 1959 and a popular shopkeeper Don Savage in 1964. After that they reverted to the dreary list of unknowns offered by party headquarters and came nowhere.

Last days of the Old Town Hall

ONE of the last functions held in the old town hall jutting into Tonbridge High Street at the entrance to Castle Street ,was the proclamation of King Edward VII in 1902.

Soon afterwards the building was demolished, but the affection which it enjoyed never transferred to its nominal replacement, the Public Hall. It became the Capitol cinema, then a leisure centre.

The old town hall, venue for most Tonbridge events, was in an advanced state of decay when the end came. It was the site of the main public water pump, and sheltered the fire brigade's escape ladder, moved there after a tragedy two years earlier (see page 76).

The Town Hall clock by a Tonbridge maker, Barcham, was preserved for years in an attic at the Castle and, as late as 1970, was pronounced by an expert to be complete. Most of it has since vanished and only the timber case and one part survive. Also lost is the curfew bell which used to be rung each evening at 8pm as a signal for people to be indoors.

Goats walked to market through a traffic-free Tonbridge High Street, widened at the turn of the century. On the right is the Bull Hotel.

Froglets' books

In The Wake of The Hurricane
(National Edition) paperback
Reprint due October 1995...........................£8.95

Surrey in The Hurricane
ISBN 0 9513019 2 6...................................£7.50

London's Hurricane
Paperback ISBN 0 9513019 3 4 ....£7.95
Hardback ISBN 0 9513019 8 5................£9.95

Eye on The Hurricane (Eastern Counties)
Paperback ISBN 0 9513019 6 9................£7.95
Hardback ISBN 0 9513019 7 7..................£11.95

King Oak of Sevenoaks A children's story
ISBN 1 872337 00 7....................................£6.95

County Weather Book Series
by Ian Currie, Mark Davison and Bob Ogley
The Kent Weather Book
ISBN 1 872337 35 X....................................£9.95

The Surrey Weather Book
Published by Frosted Earth
ISBN 0 9516710 1 4......................................£7.50

The Sussex Weather Book
ISBN 1 872337 13 9....................................£10.99

The Norfolk and Suffolk Weather Book
Paperback ISBN 1 872337 99 6...................£9.95
Hardback ISBN 1 872337 98 8..................£16.95

**The Hampshire and Isle of Wight
Weather Book**
ISBN 1 872337 20 1 ....£9.95

The Berkshire Weather Book
ISBN 1 872337 48 1....................................£9.95

Biggin on the Bump The history of the
most famous fighter station in the world
Paperback ISBN 1 872337 05 8.................£9.99
Hardback ISBN 1 872337 10 4..............£16.99

Doodlebugs and Rockets by Bob Ogley
The battle of the Flying Bombs
Paperback ISBN 1 872337 21 X.............£10.99
Hardback ISBN 1 872337 22 8................£16.95

Flying Bombs over England by H.E. Bates
The 'lost' manuscript
Hardback ISBN 1 872337 04 X...............£16.99

Kent at War 1939-1945 by Bob Ogley
Paperback ISBN 1 872337 82 1...............£10.99
Hardback ISBN 1 872337 49 X.............£16.99

Westerham and Crockham Hill in the War
by Helen Long
ISBN 1 872337 40 6...................................£8.95

**Underriver: Samuel Palmer's
Golden Valley**
ISBN 1 872337 45 7...................................£9.95

Forthcoming titles Autumn 1995:
Meridian Tonight A year's look at the news
in the south east
Surrey at War 1939-1945

All of the books listed on this page
can be ordered from:
Froglets Publications, Brasted
Chart, Westerham, Kent TN16 1LY.
Tel: 01959 562972
Fax: 01959 565365